John Lawson Stoddard

John Lawson Stoddard's lectures

Vol. 7

John Lawson Stoddard

John Lawson Stoddard's lectures
Vol. 7

ISBN/EAN: 9783337400538

Printed in Europe, USA, Canada, Australia, Japan

Cover: Foto ©Suzi / pixelio.de

More available books at **www.hansebooks.com**

JOHN L. STODDARD'S LECTURES

ILLUSTRATED AND EMBELLISHED WITH VIEWS OF THE
WORLD'S FAMOUS PLACES AND PEOPLE, BEING
THE IDENTICAL DISCOURSES DELIVERED
DURING THE PAST EIGHTEEN
YEARS UNDER THE TITLE
OF THE STODDARD
LECTURES

COMPLETE IN TEN VOLUMES

VOLUME VII

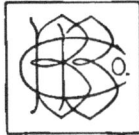

BOSTON
BALCH BROTHERS CO.
MDCCCXCVIII
CHICAGO: GEO. L. SHUMAN & CO.

THE RHINE

THE RHINE

T HE leading rivers of our globe have played a most important part in its development. They are more than mere currents of descending water. Ideas float along their surface. They have ever been the great boundaries of nations. They are the grand avenues of commerce. Their beds have been held sacred as the dwelling-places of gods. They form natural barriers to ambition, and halting-places for conquest. The destinies of mankind have, therefore, been determined by their channels. Their interest increases in proportion to the historic souvenirs which seem to mingle with their foam and murmur with their waves. In this sense one of the first among the world's great rivers is the noble Rhine. Others can boast of greater breadth and volume, a longer distance traversed to the sea, and even mightier commerce borne upon their waves; but none, except the Nile, is richer in historic memories, and even that, from its remote antiquity, cannot appeal so closely to our sympathies.

THE NOBLE RIVER.

The Rhine is the great avenue of central Europe, and on its silver thread, for seven hundred miles, are strung the pearls of love, adventure, romance, tragedy, and comedy, till one may fancy it a necklace of transcendent value, rich, like the "page of knowledge," with the "spoils of time." It is, in fact, its constant succession of beautiful and historic objects, each crowned with its appropriate legend, that gives to this great stream of Germany its matchless charm. Viewed as a river merely, the Hudson is in some respects superior to the Rhine; but add to the latter the legends and the memories of two thousand years, and the scales turn. What wonder, therefore, that the Rhine is to the Germans what the Nile was to the Egyptians, — a source of national pride and delight, a never-ending theme of song and story. Within its depths are treasures of golden memories. Let down the net of fancy at almost any point, and you can bring up gems of greater value to the world than any pearls that divers find. Two thousand years

THE CASTLE-BORDERED RHINE.

THE RHINE AT OBERWESEL.

ago its name was as well known beside the Tiber as it is now along the Hudson. Navigable for more than six hundred miles through the very heart of Europe, its dominion has been battled for throughout the centuries. Its banks have echoed to the shouts of warlike Gauls, Teutons, Romans, Franks, and Normans, and on its placid surface have been cast the shadows of the world's great conquerors and chieftains, — Cæsar, Attila, Charlemagne, Napoleon, and Von Moltke.

But to judge of the power and beauty of the Rhine one should not view it at random, but rather mark its origin and trace its growth along that path which leads it from a mountain rivulet to an imposing and majestic stream. To do this,

THE BRIDGE AT MAINZ.

we should go at the outset into the heart of Switzerland, and stand before an Alpine glacier, which, like some awful prehistoric monster, creeps forth in menace from a sea of ice, supplied from distant peaks, whose summits pierce the azure of the sky.   There is a practical as well as a poetic side to

AN ALPINE GLACIER.

these grand glaciers. They are not merely the everlasting drapery of the Alps, folding them summer and winter in their robes of ice. They are, also, the great storehouses from which the rivers of Europe are replenished ; for, from the many wounds inflicted on them by the arrows of the sun, their frigid life-blood oozes fast, forming a multitude of little torrents which finally unite to constitute one glittering stream. It is in this way that the Rhine is born. The traveler can behold it at the glacier's terminus, leaving exultingly its ice-bound cradle, as though rejoicing in the thought of freedom. The tourist must have little imagination who can stand beside this rivulet, destined to gain, erelong, such vast proportions, and not compare it to a human life : both at the start so tiny and helpless, so easily inclined in one way or another ; yet fated, later on, perhaps to win the admiration of the world, change, it may be, the history of nations, and ultimately be lost in the two oceans, — one of Time, the other of Eternity.

THE CRADLE OF THE RHINE.

A few miles farther down its course, we find the youthful river rushing on, apparently eager to prove its new-found strength and speed. Ah, river! I have often thought, you will not soon discover a safer or more lovely spot than this, your mountain-girdled home, which you are in such haste to leave. Care and responsibility will come to you soon enough; and these your sparkling waves, which can now only glitter in the sun and murmur in their shallow path, will soon bear on their breast the commerce of great cities, and roll in majesty past many

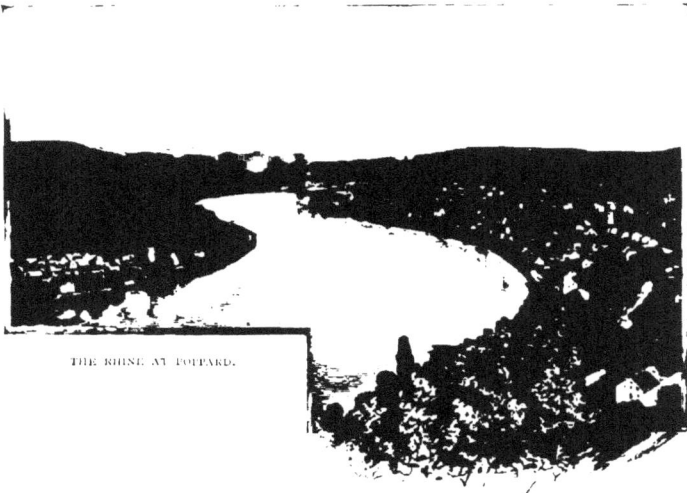

THE RHINE AT BOPPARD.

PFEIFFER'S GORGE.

a lovely meadow and em-
battled crag. What an
amount of life and history
hangs on this little crystal
thread!

Another interesting
point in the development
of the young Rhine is
where it is joined by its
first tributary. The meet-
ing-place is in the vicinity
of one of the most impressive spots in Europe,
known as "Pfeiffer's
Gorge." Through this tremendous chasm the river Tamina,
apparently in frantic haste to meet the Rhine, has worn itself
a path. On either side tower dark walls of rock, which are
not merely perpendicular, but actually bend toward each other,
so that they seem about to fall and fill the river with their
mass. On one side, a light wooden bridge clings to the

rocks, as if in fear, some
forty feet above the
stream. At first, I halted
at the entrance, afraid to
trust myself to such a
frail support; but, as I
ventured further through
the gorge, I quite forgot
where I was walking, in
admiration of the place.
Yet, for a single moment,
I was never more terrified
in my life than in that
dark ravine. When we

THE BATH OF THE TAMINA.

had entered it, quite unobserved by us, black clouds were rolling up their masses in the summer sky. Accordingly, half an
hour later, there suddenly came a blinding flash, as though the
blade of a colossal sword had been swept downward through
the gorge, and then withdrawn with inconceivable rapidity. This
was succeeded almost instantly by a terrific crash of thunder,
which fairly made our hearts stand still. Moreover, that single
peal was but the prelude to a dozen more, whose echoes, harsh
and jagged as the rocks themselves, were hurled about, from
cliff to cliff, until they seemed the screams
and laughter of malignant demons.

Soon after being reinforced by
this ally, the youthful Rhine ac-
quires an experience unlike all
others in its history, by a temporary sojourn in, and identifica-
tion with, Lake Constance. A
prize too precious for one nation
to defend seems this enchanting
inland sea; for, in its circuit of one
hundred miles, five different countries —
Bavaria, Baden, Austria, Würtemberg, and
Switzerland — encircle it like sentinels. I

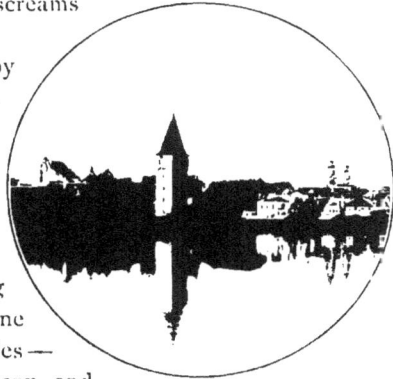

LAKE CONSTANCE.

first beheld it one evening, in 1880, when on my way to
the Passion Play at Ober-Ammergau, and I shall never cease
to think with pleasure of the magic light, which then fell
softly on the illumined shore. The lake itself lay like an
emerald shield, and, in the mirror of its peaceful flood,
a second town, the counterpart of that upon the bank, appeared to be inverted in a sea of color; while in the sunset
sky so many glorious hues were visible, that a great treas-
ure-house of Nature, filled with materials for a million rain-
bows, appeared to have been broken open, and its prismatic
colors scattered broadcast.

Upon a gently sloping hill above Lake Constance is an old-fashioned, modest country-house, which several times within the present century has stood forth prominently on the political background, not alone of France, but of the whole of Europe. It is the Château of Arenenberg, for years the home of Josephine's daughter, Queen Hortense, and her son Napoleon III.

THE CHÂTEAU OF ARENENBERG

It was in 1817, while Napoleon was still a captive at St. Helena, that Hortense, exiled from France by the decision of the allied Powers, came to this quiet resting-place, hoping to end her troubled life with a few years of such tranquil happiness, as it had not yet been her fortune to enjoy.

Here, in her exile, that devoted mother welcomed as guests the famous men, who, during the first empire, had filled the world with their renown; and they, in turn, in this comparatively humble home of the ex-Queen of Holland, loved to recall the triumphs of their Emperor, and tell the stories of his wonderful campaigns. This château, therefore, was a school for Louis Napoleon's ambition; and since it was from this, his mother's residence, that he went forth to become President of the French Republic, and finally the acknowledged sovereign of France, Arenenberg may be regarded as the starting-point of that astonishing political

THE BOUDOIR OF HORTENSE.

cycle, in which Napoleon the Little strove to imitate Napoleon the Great.

One summer, several years ago, I visited this mansion of Napoleonic memories, and was admitted to what had been the boudoir of Queen Hortense. It seemed as if she still must be residing here, for everything recalled her presence. Her portrait hung upon the wall; the writing-desk she used stood in its accustomed place; and near it was the harp her skillful hands had often waked to melody. The musical accomplishments of Hortense were remarkable, and it was she who composed the words and music of that celebrated melody which has become one of the national airs of France: *Partant pour la Syrie.*

In a pretty chapel near the château is a kneeling marble

THE CHAPEL OF ARENENBURG.

statue, upon the pedestal of which is the simple inscription,
"To Queen Hortense, by her son Napoleon III." There is a
look of patient resignation on the sculptured face, well suited
to the character of her whom it represents; for her brave and
uncomplaining spirit rose above her trials with such heroism
as to force admiration of her character even from her enemies.
Napoleon frequently exclaimed of her, "Hortense makes me
believe in virtue." As a child, she had seen her father die
upon the guillotine amid the horrors of the Revolution; a
maiden, she had at the command of her mother sacrificed her
own affections to a political marriage which had proved one
long agony to endure; a mother, she had lost the dearly loved
child whom Napoleon intended to make his heir, and whose

STATUE OF HORTENSE

little life had been
the only barrier
to the divorce of
Josephine; a
queen, she had
watched the
hopes and for-
tunes of herself
and friends go
down in ruin with
the empire; a
daughter, she
had seen her
mother die bro-
ken-hearted at
Malmaison, and
Napoleon wear
out his life in anguish on the barren rock of St. Helena. What wonder, then, that wearied of the past and
almost hopeless of the future she often sought relief in
prayer?

Leaving the château, I lingered in its pretty garden. Here, seated in the shade of the historic trees whose branches had so often sheltered the daughter and the grandchild of Josephine, I realized the fact that truth is sometimes stranger than the wildest fiction. For, when the star of Napoleon had apparently forever sunk behind the sea-girt rock of St. Helena, a youth, whose only fortune was the fact that he bore his uncle's name, sat here and dreamed of an empire that he would one day rule. Through intrigue, chance, and the notorious *coup d'état* of 1851, that dream was

THE GARDEN AT ARENENBERG.

realized; but the empire, after enduring twenty years, went down in shame and exile; and now, when all is changed, to this château, so haunted with sad memories, the ex-Empress Eugénie, its present owner, still occasionally comes, to wander sadly through its solitudes, throneless, childless, and a widow.

The Rhine is cosmopolitan. It is not satisfied to linger in a single country. The narrow boundaries of Switzerland cannot contain its rapidly expanding volume. Hence, leaving soon the land of its nativity, it enters Germany, to which thenceforth its splendor and its fame belong. It is, however, changed. Its sojourn in Lake Constance, which is of enormous depth, has had that influence upon the river which education and experience impress upon a youth. Its character, like its river-bed, seems to have deepened and broadened. It moves more steadily and with less uproar and excitement. It has gained power and volume; but it will need them both, for it is about to encounter trial and resistance. As if it had received warning of the approaching struggle, the river, at some distance from the town, seems to be making preparation for the coming conflict. Its waves grow agitated, and its current swifter. A murmur of defiance rises from its depths.

THE RHINE ABOVE SCHAFFHAUSEN.

Whatever is to be the trial, we plainly see that the young Rhine will meet it like a hero. At last the crisis comes; for, at Schaffhausen, Nature, as if to test the strength of her ambitious child, has reared directly in its path a monstrous ledge of rock, three hundred feet in width. It is useless! With a shout of triumph in its leap for life the Rhine bounds over the cliff, falls eighty-five feet, extricates itself from the seething depths below, shakes from its brow a billion glittering drops, which sparkle in the sun like clouds of diamonds, and sweeps along unharmed and free. It is plain that there has been a conflict. The few remaining rocks that

THE FALLS OF SCHAFFHAUSEN.

still oppose the river stand like grim veterans who have thus far managed to survive the onset, while scores of their companions have long since disappeared from view, their huge, dismembered bodies buried in the triumphant stream.

But our sympathy is not with them. It is rather with the freedom-seeking Rhine, which will bear no restraint, and hurls itself against the enemy with a roar of anger and a shout of victory that can be heard for miles. Yet, this is not for every traveler a place of romance ; or even if it be, the terribly prosaic claims of hunger and of thirst inevitably silence, for a time, his dreams and fancies. Thus, in the hotel register at Schaffhausen are these practical lines, composed by one who certainly did not believe in total abstinence :

"THE FREEDOM-SEEKING RHINE."

" As I stood just now by the Falls of the Rhine,
 I was suddenly seized with a fancy divine;
 And I thought to myself — if these Falls of the Rhine
 Instead of water, were only wine,
 I should certainly choose them for falls of mine."

A few hours after leaving Schaffhausen, the traveler in Rhineland reaches, by a trifling détour, the former paradise of gamblers, and the still charming health resort, — Baden-Baden.

A GLIMPSE OF BADEN-BADEN.

It were folly to pass this unnoticed. I have been sometimes asked, by persons planning a European tour, " What would you recommend as the best halting-place within the limits of southwestern Germany, if you were pressed for time, and could select but one place on the way to Switzerland?" To such a question I always answer, " Baden-Baden." It is true, to do so is selecting from a great embarrassment of riches, but I am sure the choice of Baden-Baden will not be regretted. Nevertheless, in judging of a place, how much depends upon the accidents of health and weather! A rainy day, a sleepless night, an insolent waiter, or an attempt at extortion, — any one or all of these may tinge the fairest place with gloom; and, even under favorable circumstances, how many lovely scenes are spoiled for us through some mistake which, if we had been warned of it, might just as well have been avoided! The warning to be

BADEN-BADEN.

given in respect to Baden-Baden is this: Do not select for
your abode a hotel far from the music, gaiety, and beauty of
its famous park; for that is the centre of its
festivities, the spot where
the pulse of Baden-
Baden beats most
rapidly. To be
remote from this,
to hear its music
merely at a dis-
tance, to see the
promenaders only
when you walk
from your hotel to
do so, is quite as

THE THEATRE.

undesirable as a poor seat in a theatre, where you discern
only a portion of the stage, and lose the language of the
actors. But how is one to find a home within this charming
neighborhood? This was the question which we asked ourselves on the first
morning after our
arrival; as, discon-
tented with our rooms,
we had approached
the park, half tempted
to abandon Baden, if
we could not secure
some situation nearer
to this field of mer-
riment. At length we
saw an attractive
building, just across
the street from it,
which did not some-

THE RESTAURANT.

how have the air of a hotel, although two gentlemen were taking breakfast in the garden, and a sleek waiter (the inevitable napkin on his arm) was standing on the steps. Upon the wall, however, was the inscription, " Maison Messmer." " Could we but find rooms here," whispered a member of the party, " we would remain two months, at least." Approaching the waiter, therefore, he inquired, " Pardon me, is this a hotel ? " " *Ja wohl, mein Herr.*" He glanced at us triumphantly, but we discreetly turned away our heads. " Are there any rooms to let at present ? " he continued in a voice which trembled from excitement. "*Das glaube ich ganz wohl. Kommen Sie herein, meine Herrschaften.* I will speak to Herr Messmer." A moment more and the proprietor appeared. Best and kindest of all landlords, we little thought that morning, now so long ago, of the warm friendship which would soon arise between us, strengthened by every annual visit, and undiminished by the lapse of years. Too modest to proclaim the fact himself, we subsequently learned that he was highly esteemed by old Kaiser William and the Empress, had been the recipient of several presents from them, and was among the guests invited to their golden wedding in Berlin. In fact, it was in this very hotel that both the Kaiser and his wife invariably passed a few weeks every year. Informed of this by the waiter, while Herr Mess-

THE HOTEL MESSMER.

mer himself had
for a moment dis-
appeared, we held
a hurried consul-
tation. Could we,
by any possibility,
remain in this oc-
casional abode of
royalty? Would
not the prices
also be "royal"?
They did not
prove to be so.
Indeed, we soon
discovered that,

IN THE ALLÉE AT BADEN.

when not occupied by the imperial family, the Maison
Messmer was no more expensive than any other hostelry.
Accordingly, we hired rooms at once, and stepping out
upon our balconies surveyed the scene before us. It was
enchanting. On all sides were graceful hills, dark with the
splendid foliage of the Black Forest, from which, at frequent

THE PARK, "CONVERSATION HOUSE," AND
HOTEL MESSMER.

THE MUSIC-STAND.

intervals, in striking contrast to their sombre background, emerged, to glitter in the sun, the white walls of some pretty villa. One was the residence of a Russian prince, who, long before the frozen arms of the river Neva release St. Petersburg from their prolonged embrace, forgets here, amid opening flowers and the songs of birds, the chill and gloom of Russia's capital.

In the foreground, so near, in fact, that I could toss a coin into it from my balcony, was the Casino Park, lined on one side with an enticing restaurant and the "Conversation House," and on the other with a row of tempting shops. In front of these stood the pretty music-stand, where, three times a day, at early morning, afternoon, and evening, a well-

IN THE "CONVERSATION HOUSE."

trained orchestra affords enjoyment to attentive listeners.
An Oriental sovereign, well versed in pleasures, once decreed
that he should always be awakened by music. How often
had I thought of that as one of the most exquisite of luxuries,
which I should never know! But here, in Baden-Baden, we
experienced it. It is a special feature of the Hotel Messmer,
which stamps itself in-
delibly upon the mem-
ory. Each morn-
ing, about seven
o'clock, we would
be gradually
roused to con-
sciousness by
the inspiring
harmonies of a
German choral;
and then, for a
full hour, half sleep-
ing, half awake, we
would enjoy a concert,
just far enough removed to

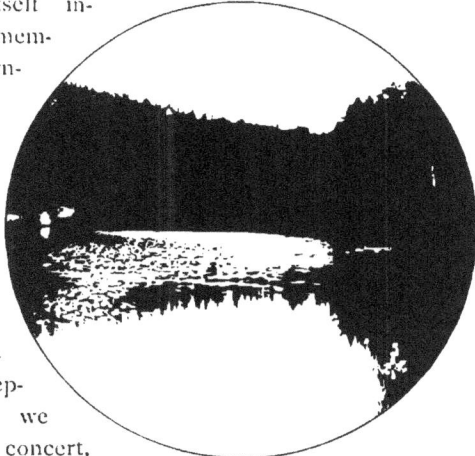

THE WALDSEE.

make its strains seem echoes from the realm of dreamland,
just near enough to let us lose no portion of its melodies.
"But, if the weather be rainy," it may be asked, "are you de-
prived of music?" By no means. The visitor, in such a case,
may leave his hotel balcony and enter the "Conversation
House," to find himself in a superbly decorated hall, where
dazzling chandeliers rival sunlight, and waxed floors tempt
visitors to dance in rhythm to the music of the orchestra,
which has come in from the pavilion. Very different, however, was the scene displayed here thirty years ago. The
"Conversation House" was then the famous "gambling hell"
of Baden, where green baize tables and the fascinating

roulette-wheel lured thousands of the butterflies of wealth and
fashion to their ruin, like moths to a flame. But now, since
gambling is no longer allowed, Baden-Baden has become vir-
tuous by compulsion. Despite its loss, however, the place is
still attractive. The beauty of its situation, the healing proper-
ties of its springs, its lovely park, and the adjoining forest draw
admiring thou-
sands to enjoy
the scenery, and
listen to the
charming music
which, hour after
hour, floats upon
the air. The only
persons who told
me they regretted
the prohibition
of gaming were
the shop-keepers,
who, naturally
enough, desire
the good old

THE OLD GAMING-HALL.

times when fortunes, made or lost in a night, were spent with
fabulous rapidity.

One can hardly imagine how gay and animated is
the scene on which the tourist gazes from the windows
of the Hotel Messmer, especially at night. The long,
brilliant avenue is then filled with promenaders, the chairs
on either side are occupied, waiters flit about, dispensing
light refreshments, and during the pauses in the music
the air is filled with the hum of conversation. Seated at
such a time upon the private balcony of your room, you
look down on that scene, as on the stage from a pro-
scenium box, able to view and listen to it all with perfect

HORNBERG IN THE BLACK FOREST.

ease, and, literally, if you choose, attired in dressing-gown and slippers.

It must be acknowledged, however, that, since the Franco-Prussian War, the gay and fashionable life of Baden has largely disappeared. The place still remains delightful, but it no longer effervesces like champagne. Parisians do not visit it as formerly, and write sarcastically of the change from French to German cus-toms. One witty writer, for exam-ple, says that now, instead of snowy shoulders, sparkling eyes, and charming cos-tumes, one sees here gouty Ger-mans l i m p i n g along the prom-enade, supported by their patient *fraus*, or gathered in the " Conversa-

THE RIVER OOS.

tion House," like cabbages raised under glass ; and that, in-stead of the gay rivalry of spendthrifts, who bought all kinds of trinkets at the shops, the wretched salesmen are once or twice a day aroused from sleep, by some huge-waisted Hol-lander, who bargains with them half an hour for a pair of stock-ings ! All this, of course, is caricature, yet Baden must have had in former times a charm of which we see few traces now. The loveliest summer toilettes were then inaugurated here. It was the accepted ball-room of all Europe, — the garden of Paris, — the promenade of England. Then, in the balmy summer evenings, these music-haunted paths became the ren-

THE PROMENADE OF THE DRINKING HALL.

dezvous of friends who had last met at Nice or on the Paris boulevards, and in these winding avenues Love reigned supreme and held his court unchallenged, and here, if anywhere, "at lovers' vows of constancy Jove laughed."

Not far from the "Conversation House" is the Drinking Hall, a handsome structure, nearly three hundred feet in length, whose noble portico,

THE DRINKING HALL.

adorned with frescos representing the legends of the Black
Forest, make it a most agreeable promenade for those who
come here for the cure.   In the rotunda of the edifice rises
the celebrated spring of Baden-Baden, the virtues of which
have been sung for centuries.   As its waters have a temperature of about one hundred and fifty degrees Fahrenheit,

DAS ALTE SCHLOSS.

it is not surprising that such a covered gallery has
been provided, where invalids can walk, and wait with
patience till the liquid cools.   It may perhaps console them to
remember that, nearly two thousand years ago, people were
doing here precisely the same thing.   For when the building
was in process of construction, extensive relics of Roman baths
were discovered, proving that those old conquerors of the world
had learned the efficacy of this spring, and had erected their
votive tablets to the gods.

Whenever I was seated at my window in the Hotel Messmer,
if I looked off beyond the town, I saw, three miles away, a ruin
of enormous size, crowning the summit of a wooded mountain.

It is known as *Das alte Schloss,* or the Old Castle, and was the residence of the lords of Baden, who in the Middle Ages ruled this region with a rod of iron. Two hundred years ago the French dismantled it, and then, for half a century at least, it lay neglected in the forest solitude. But now a visit to the Old Castle is the favorite excursion to be made from Baden, and every pleasant afternoon, a score of tourists, who have ap-

THE GATEWAY.

proached it by long walks or drives completely shaded by gigantic trees, may be seen standing on its ruined walls, gazing with delight upon the scene below. The entrance to this castle is a narrow portal beyond which one can see a winding passage, resembling a street in an old Oriental town. The outer gate was only the first of many similar portals which followed one another, like successive doors in a safe-deposit vault. A handful of determined men could easily, therefore, have resisted here an army of invaders; for, in addition to the ponderous gates, the walls were pierced with narrow loop-holes, through which the garrison could with safety fire upon the enemy. To-day, how great the transformation! The massive walls are roofless now, and visitors may enter fearlessly a corridor, which, no doubt, in the period of the castle's glory, frequently echoed to the clang of arms and tramp of horses' feet. Where mailed

THE ENTRANCE

watchmen stood
guard, a peasant
woman keeps a
booth of trinkets;
and, on an ancient
tower, the trav-
eler, wearied by
his mountain
climb, beholds
the touching
legend, "Res-
taurant." It is ap-
propriate that be-
neath this word
there should, also,

be inscribed an arrow; for swiftly as a feathered barb does every
German, at least, glide through the adjoining doorway to order
beer, coffee, butter-brod, and sausage, without which no excursion

seems to him
complete, nor
even an after-
noon endurable.

Many war-
like deeds are
said to have
been performed
in ancient times
in and about
the Old Castle,
but it is not
necessary to go
into antiquity
for thrilling
scenes con-

THE BANQUET HALL IN THE OLD CASTLE.

nected with its history. One day, as we were climbing to the highest portion of the building by some rock-hewn steps, Herr Messmer told us of a tragic incident of which he had been personally cognizant. When gambling prevailed at Baden, almost as many suicides took place in the Black Forest as now occur at Monaco. Among the· visitors here, in 1863,

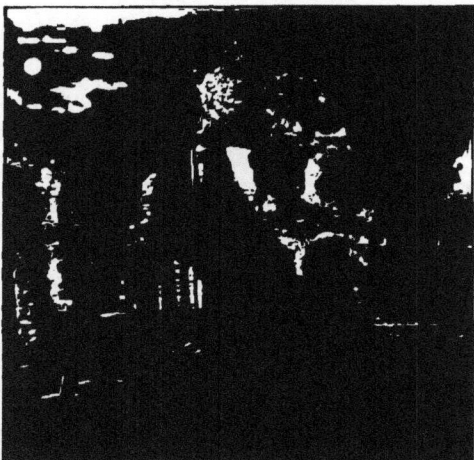

RUINED WALLS.

were a young Russian officer and the lady of his love. They had eloped from Moscow. Their funds had become exhausted. The money on which the young man counted was refused him, save on condition that he left his friend and came back to his family alone. Unwilling to do this, in his despair the officer tempted fortune at the gaming-table. In vain! In one brief hour he had lost the little money that remained to him. Leaving the brilliant hall, he plunged directly into the Black Forest, and made his way to this castle. It was a glorious night, and moonlight lent enchantment to the place; but its beauty offered him no consolation. Meanwhile, alarmed at his delay, suspecting his design, and acting upon the information given her by a servant, the lady followed breathless in his footsteps. Again and again, in the darkness of the wood, she called his name, but met with no response. At last, when she had dragged her trembling

limbs almost to
the entrance of
the castle, a pis-
tol-shot rang out
upon the air.
Half-frenzied,
with recovered
strength, she
bounded up the
ruined battle-
ments, to find her
lover dead beside
the wall. She
did not hesitate
a moment. Press-

A CORRIDOR IN THE CASTLE.

ing a farewell kiss upon his lips, still moist and warm, she
took the pistol from his hand and in an instant more fell
lifeless by his side.

It is, of course, for the interest of the people of Baden
to make the place as beautiful and inviting as possible.
Accordingly, the authorities leave nothing undone to render
it attractive. In addition to its magnificent bathing establish-

ment, and the Casino Park with its frequent concerts, illu-
minations, and select entertainments, the town itself resembles
a lovely garden, in which a long avenue called the Lichtenthal Allée forms a delightful promenade, adorned with fountains, flowers, and shade trees,
among which flows the little
river Oos, spanned by a multitude of pretty bridges, and
bordered by superb hotels and

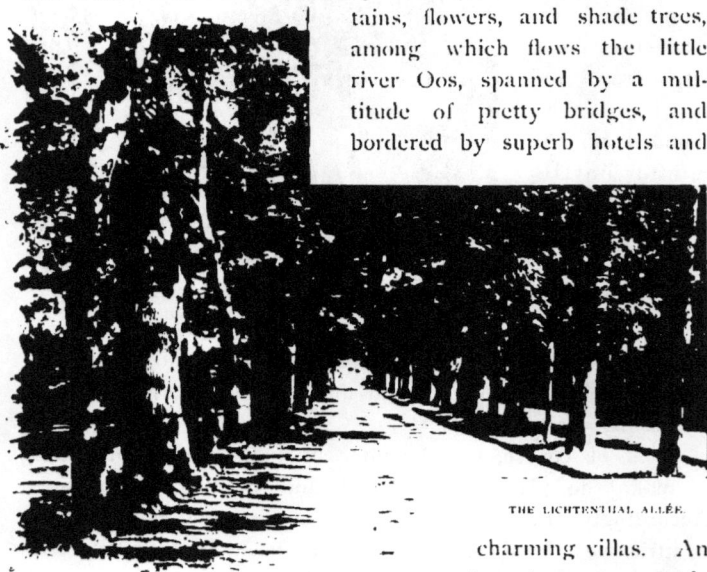

THE LICHTENTHAL ALLÉE.

charming villas.   An
attempt was once made
on this promenade to assassinate old Emperor William.   One
day, when he was walking here, a miserable wretch sprang
from behind a tree, aimed a pistol at him and fired.   Instead of hitting him, however, the bullet entered one of
the adjoining elms.   The tree, in consequence, came very
near suffering the fate of the famous willow which over-
hung Napoleon's grave at St. Helena, — that of being
carried away piecemeal by relic hunters.   Accordingly, the
town authorities encased its trunk in a stout coat of canvas,
painted black.   But even this did not suffice.   The tourists'
knives cut through the canvas and attacked the tree.   Herr

Messmer then suggested the idea of covering the two adjoining trees also with canvas. This plan proved perfectly successful, for strangers, being at a loss to know which tree was the historic elm, gave up all hope of relics, and retired in confusion.

One of the charms of Baden-Baden, which has drawn me thither summer after
summer, has
been the
great variety
of forest
drives and
walks in its vi-
cinity. Thus,
within a few
hundred feet
of the Casino
Park, you can
enter the
Black Forest
and stroll
for miles be-
neath impos-
ing trees on
paths which,
for a con-
siderable dis-
tance from
the town, are
carefully
swept every
day by old
women.

It is necessary to see a German forest to comprehend its beauty. Before I went to Germany I had little idea of what a well-kept forest was; but after spending a few delightful days in the Thuringian and Black Forests, the many German songs and poems which describe them were readily understood and heartily appreciated.

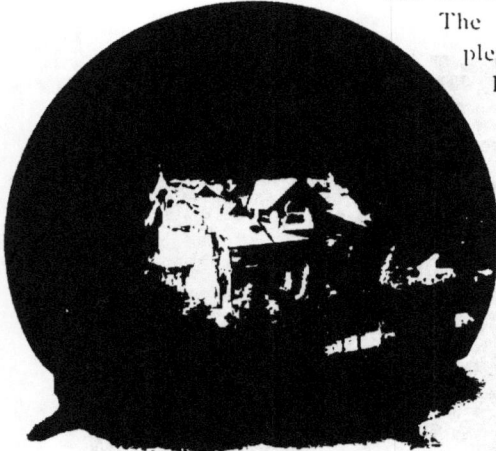

IN THE BLACK FOREST.

The Black Forest, for example, on the edge of which Baden-Baden is situated, is ninety miles in length and twenty-five in breadth, and tourists can drive through it on finely graded, macadamized roads, amid thousands of majestic trees, which foresters keep free from underbrush and useless limbs; while, here and there, a ruined monastery or romantic castle cuts its profile sharply on the sombre background. Moreover, trailing in and out, like silver threads among the stately pines, are little streams which fill the air with freshness and the cadence of a song. What wonder, then, that no part of Europe is richer in poetic legends than the Schwarzwald? Books have been written merely to describe them; a hundred castle walls preserve them still in fresco, or in tapestry; and the quaint dwarfs and giants, princesses and fairies, of whom we read with bated breath in childhood, were all of German origin, and usually played their parts for good or ill within the limits of this forest.

It is not long ago that the good, simple-minded people

of this region firmly believed that these dark-hued pines were
once inhabited by golden-haired sirens, so fair and white that
they seemed born of the water-lilies, and that, when the moonbeams turned by their
caress the surface of
the rivers to a silver
pavement, those fair
nymphs danced there-
on the whole night
long, until the first
pale streak of day
came glimmering
in the east, when
they would van-
ish like a dream.
Absurd, of course,
these legends
seem to-day; yet
who will deny
that, in a poetic
sense at least, the
world is poorer
by their loss?

THE RUINS OF ALL SAINTS.

Hidden away from the world, in the cool depths of the
Black Forest, within the shade of stately trees and within
easy distance of some beautiful cascades, is the once famous
monastery of All Saints. That all who lived within its walls
were saints, I would not venture to affirm; but it was certainly
a noble building in its prime, five hundred years ago, and held

its place as one of the richest institutions of the kind in Germany. At the very beginning of this century, however, its property was confiscated and the site abandoned. A miserable fortune then awaited the monastery, since it was purchased

HEIDELBERG.

for a cotton-mill. Apparently the gods protected it from sacrilege; for, on the very day when its new owners were to take possession, the lightning's bolt set fire to the massive edifice and made of it the ruin which we see. No lover of the beautiful, however, can regret it; for now, instead of a prosaic factory, the tourist finds in this delightful spot one of the finest ruins to which luxuriant ivy and romantic legends ever lent their charm.

Soon after leaving Baden-

THE CASTLE ON THE RHINE.

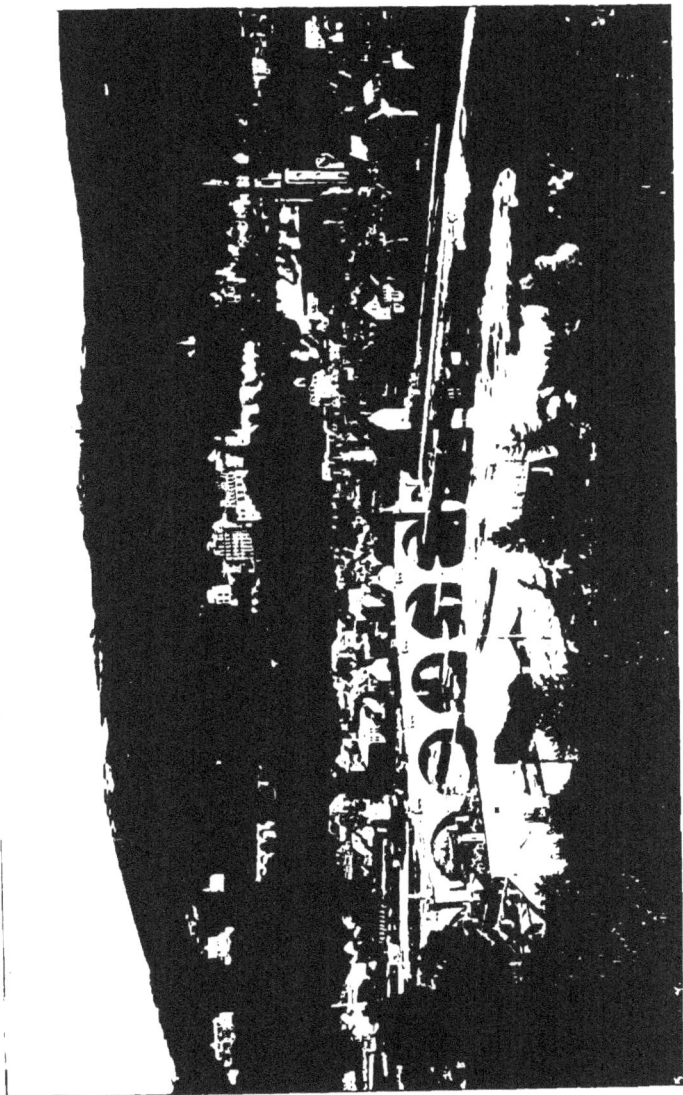

HEIDELBERG FROM THE RHINE

Baden, another charming feature of the Rhineland greets the traveler in Heidelberg, partially mirrored in the river Neckar, which here rolls downward like a flood of silver to the Rhine some miles away. The great attraction of the place is, of course, its famous castle, which is certainly one of the grandest strongholds ever designed by mediæval architects, and has been enthusiastically called the "Alhambra of Germany." All German castles are picturesquely located, but few can equal this; for the steep mountain side of Heidelberg is covered with a dense forest, from which, more than three hundred feet above the river, the lovely ruin emerges, like a solitary flower

HEIDELBERG PARK.

out of a mass of dark green leaves. It is only a short walk from the Castle Hotel to this historic edifice, but it will not be easily forgotten; for the dark woods are threaded with a multitude of winding paths, completely sheltered from the sun, and in the early spring bordered with violets. Sometimes these walks are spanned with ruined arches, adorned with wild flowers, and caressed by the clinging fingers of innumerable vines. Moreover, in these sylvan shades, on every pleasant summer afternoon, the visitor can seat himself in a rustic café (the roof of which is the green canopy of the trees), and listen to orchestral music, that invariable feature of German out-door life, cheering the pilgrimage of the summer tourist in Rhineland with continuous strains of melody.

On entering the courtyard of the castle, we see a great variety of architecture in the buildings that enclose it.

A CORNER IN THE COURTYARD.

Each differs from its neighbor, both in general design and ornamentation, for Heidelberg Castle was not the work of a single architect, or even of one age, but is, rather, a series of palaces built by successive princes during a period of three hundred years. A wonderfully fascinating place is this old courtyard, either at sunset, when its ruined walls, with their elaborate statues and stone-carving, stand out like finely decorated screens against the sky, or, when the moon pours a flood of silver through their ruined arches, giving a glory to their remnants of departed splendor, and softening all traces of the conflict which they still survive. In that mysterious light their sculptured kings and warriors seem like living beings, who have assembled to converse of the old times when the grand halls were filled with valiant knights, fair ladies, and sweet-voiced minstrels.

No one can fail to be impressed with the former strength of the castle's walls, if he observes an enormous

THE COURTYARD OF HEIDELBERG CASTLE.

mass of masonry called the "over-thrown tower." Two hundred years ago, the army of Louis XIV. left the town of Heidelberg a smoldering heap of ruins, and the castle itself so far dismantled, that the French king ordered a medal to be struck, bearing the inscription, "Heidelberg is destroyed." But,

STATUE-COVERED WALLS.

happily, it was impossible to destroy such a massive structure, and some of its old battlements remain almost as strong as formerly in their enormous thickness of twenty feet.

A HISTORIC FAÇADE.

The presence of ivy, in connection with the ruins of the past, is one of the most beautiful and suggestive sights in nature. It is also a peculiarity of the North. Egyptian ruins stand in the burning sunlight, desolate and naked, with all the blows they have received from time and their

SCULPTURED KINGS AND WARRIORS.

despoilers plainly visible ; but in the lands of mist and snow, ruins are quickly covered with a lovely mantle of protection. How tenderly the ivy touches the broken outlines of their stony features, putting its tiny tendrils forth, like an infant's fingers creeping over a mother's face! And when the union of the vine and ruin is completed, how sturdily those rootlets cling to every coign of vantage, and enter every nook and cranny, until by the sheer force of numbers their lilliputian hands screen and apparently support the massive walls! Is it not owing to its ivied cloak that many an ancient structure is more beautiful in ruin than when perfect? And who can stand by such an edi-

A RHENISH RUIN.

fice, made lovelier by vines which never would have come to it but for misfortune, and not reflect how character is often beautified by adversity, developing in trial a multitude of noble traits which in prosperity would never have been seen? Something is wanting in a man who has not known misfortune. To have really lived one must have suffered.

In the cellar of the castle is the largest wine-cask in the world, which is no less than twenty-four feet high, and has a capacity of more than a quar-

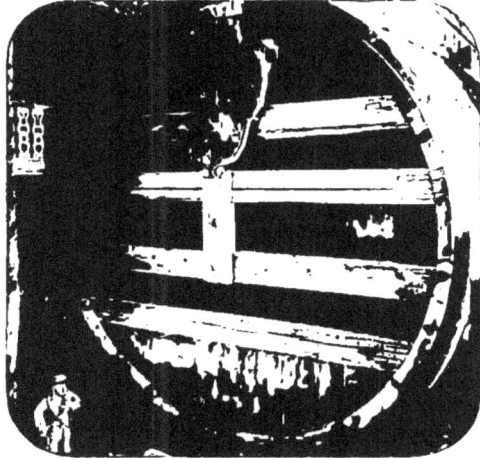

THE GREAT WINE-CASK.

ter of a million bottles of wine. In olden times, when this huge tun had been filled with the produce of the vintage, a dance took place upon the platform that surmounts it, and the old castle walls resounded to gay music, songs, and laughter; but ever since 1769 the cask has held no wine, and the days of Heidelberg's festivities are gone forever.

There are three modes of traveling on the Rhine. The first and fastest is, of course, the railway; but this, while good for business purposes, is rarely taken by the tourist. The second is the steamboat, which is both rapid and agreeable. The third and last is the long line of splendid carriage-roads which wind around the bases of the mountains and skirt the borders of the

A CHOICE OF ROUTES.

stream. Ninety-nine out of every hundred travelers, probably, take the steamboat journey, and thus glide rapidly in one day past the famous Rhenish villages and castles; but this is like going through a picture-gallery on roller-skates. There is no time on such a trip really to observe anything. The most delightful way to travel through Rhineland is in a carriage, or on foot. Of this I was convinced, some years ago, in talking with a gentleman who had made such a tour. I had myself sailed up and down the Rhine a number of times, and thought I knew it tolerably well; but when we came to speak of some details, I found that, com-

ALONG THE RHINE.

pared with my companion, I knew very little. "How is this?"
I inquired, in some chagrin, when he had asked my impressions of a place I had not seen, "how is it possible that you
know the entire route so perfectly?"   "It is easily explained,"
was the reply.   "I recently hired a carriage and a pair of
horses, and, with my son, drove leisurely along the Rhine
for a hundred and fifty miles, having no end of good hotels
in which to eat when we were hungry, and sleep when we
were weary.   Journeying thus, we halted when and where
we liked, observed the village life, and visited leisurely the
ruins, which, looked on from the steamer at a distance, merely
produce a vague impression soon to be forgotten."   I contem-
plated him with admiration, not unmixed with envy. No one
could have called him an extensive traveler.   He had not been
in Egypt, Spain, or even Italy, but he had done at least
one thing in Europe thoroughly,— he had seen the Rhine.

The usual starting-point for a sail down the Rhine is Mainz,
or, as the French prefer to say, Mayence.   This, if not beautiful, is nevertheless a town of great historical celebrity.   It was
one of the old Roman strongholds built along the Rhine ; and,

A RHENISH CASTLE.

shortly before the birth of Christ, the Roman general, Drusus,
built across the river at this point a bridge of stone. Since
then poor Mainz has been repeatedly the spoil of conquerors,
from Attila to Bonaparte. Yet, though its annals have been
often stained with blood, its greatest fame comes from a very
different source. In its chief public square stands a monument
made from the designs of the Danish sculptor, Thorwaldsen,
and erected by
subscriptions
from all parts of
Europe. It is the
statue of the most
illustrious citizen
of Mainz, John
Gutenberg, who
here invented
movable types,
and whose first
printing-office, oc-
cupied by him in
1443, is still pre-
served. Unfortu-
nately, like many
of the benefactors
of his race, Guten-

STATUE OF GUTENBERG AT MAINZ.

berg died friendless and in want. Nevertheless, among the
heroes of the Rhineland, his name stands out in characters
that will forevermore command the admiration of posterity; and
although Cæsar, Charlemagne, Napoleon, and many lesser warriors have played their rôles in the historic drama of this river,
—leaving behind them memories which are now inseparable from
the stream itself, — the man, whose life-work revolutionized the
world and helped mankind immeasurably onward in its upward
path, was one who neither held a sword nor wore a crown.

MAINZ FROM THE BRIDGE.

As the swift steamer bears the tourist down the Rhine from Mainz, a charming feature soon reveals itself in the extensive vineyards glistening in the sun. Sometimes the shores are lined with them for miles. The most renowned and valuable lie upon the slopes of the Johannisberg. This mountain was formerly the property of an Austrian statesman, Metternich. It is well known that, in addition to his love for vineyards and diplomacy, Metternich had a mania for collecting autographs, and his relations during thirty years with the sovereigns of Europe (some of whom owed to him their crowns) had naturally given him a fine array of royal

CASTLE OF JOHANNISBERG.

signatures. Not content with these, however, he solicited those of persons distinguished in any walk of life. Among others, therefore, he requested the autograph of Jules Janin, a famous wit and journalist of Paris. On receiving the request, Janin immediately seized a pen and wrote :

" Paris, 15th May, 1838. — Received from Prince Metternich, twenty-four bottles of his best Johannisberg wine.   (Signed) JULES JANIN."

The wit was well appreciated and rewarded, for in a month the journalist received from Metternich the two dozen bottles of

Johannisberg. It is probable, however, that Metternich kept the signature of the witty Frenchman longer than Janin kept the sparkling wine of Metternich.

Oh, the amount of labor that has been expended on the Rhenish hillsides! Without man's ingenuity, no cultivation of the grape on their steep sides would have been possible. But human skill has changed them into hanging gardens, by means of countless terraces which hold the soil that otherwise would be washed down to the river in a dozen rainstorms. We sometimes think the building of stone walls on old New England farms remarkable, but that is nothing to what has been accomplished on the Rhine. Literally, thousands of miles of carefully constructed and cemented walls, from eight to twenty feet in height, have been built along these hillsides, dividing the whole area into little vineyards (perhaps no more than twenty-five feet wide), which in places rise in thirty or forty terraces to the very summit of the mountains. Sometimes

A RHENISH HILLSIDE.

the slope is so precipitous that the soil in which the vines are planted has to be kept in baskets to retain it, and much of the soil, and all the dressing it receives, must be carried up the hills upon the shoulders of the laborers.

Soon after leaving Mainz, we find ourselves within the region of ruined castles, tenanted only by the genii of the past. From time to time old crumbling walls, or solitary towers, cast their dark silhouettes upon the sky, — some bleak and bare, others concealing their defects with vines and leaves, like Spanish beggars in their tattered mantles.

Many of these castles were formerly the abodes of men who lived by levying duties on the commerce of the river.

A BIT OF RHINELAND.

Like vultures, from their eyries, they watched the boats descend the stream, and if the tribute they demanded was refused them, they promptly attacked the crew, and secured the cargo for themselves.

Among the strongest residences of these robber barons, and even now the largest ruin on the river, is the Rheinfels. Its record is remarkable, for it was the greed and cruelty of the master of this fortress which finally drove his victims to resistance. A league was formed by several Rhenish cities to do away with this unbearable oppression ; and under that confederation, the haughty castles one by one went down. It was a bloody task. This stronghold, in particular, withstood a siege

of fifteen months
and drove back
from its battle-
ments an army
of twenty-four
thousand men;
but, finally, its
power was de-
stroyed. Nature
has charitably
thrown over these
blood-stained
walls a robe of
verdure like a
mantle of obliv-

THE RHEINFELS.

ion, and they are now the peaceful home of birds and flowers,
which fill the historic courts with song and fragrance. Best
of all, the commerce of the Rhine, to-day, sails fearlessly
beneath the gloomy towers which threatened once its ruin.

Conspicuous
among the castles
whose towers
fling their shad-
ows on the placid
bosom of this
river is the Rhein-
stein. Its origin
is lost in obscur-
ity, but there is
evidence that it
has kept watch
and ward above
the Rhine for at
least six hundred

THE RHEINSTEIN.

years. To-day, it is a summer residence of the German Emperor, and, in accordance with his wish, is kept as far as
possible in the old style. The walls, for example, are hung
with ancient armor, the windows are of stained glass, great
shaggy skins adorn the inlaid floor, and even the furniture is
antique, collected from old castles or mediæval convents.

Another prominent ruin attracting one's attention on this
journey is the
castle of Ehren-
fels. It is in
reality no older
than the Rhein-
stein, but, in its
mutilated condi-
tion, it seems
much more an-
cient. On the
occasion of my
visit, I clambered
up a staircase
in the tower
and looked out
through the case-

THE INTERIOR OF THE RHEINSTEIN.

ments near the top. The guardian of the place was a plump
German matron of such ample girth, that she did not venture
to follow me up the stairs; fearing perhaps the fate of the
watchman's wife, whose home was in the top of one of these
narrow towers, and who there grew so stout that she could
neither get down the steps, nor out of the window. When,
therefore, her husband died his successor was obliged to marry
the widow in her prison.

Not far away one sees upon a tongue of land a tall square
tower, which, although fully as old as that of Ehrenfels, was
handsomely restored in 1856. The curious legend which

adheres to it has stamped forever on its walls the title of the "Mouse Tower." For who does not remember the story of Bishop Hatto, who, in a year of famine, locked a multitude of women and children in one of his barns and set it on fire?

EHRENFELS.

"There," he exclaimed, as he saw the flames, "I have burned up a lot of miserable rats that were good for nothing but to eat corn." Hardly had he uttered the words, when a servant came running to him and announced that thousands of rats were coming that way. In terror, the bishop hastened to this tower and, barring every hole and window, thought himself secure; but in vain!

> "In at the windows, and in at the door,
> And through the walls by thousands they pour,
> And down through the ceiling and up through the floor,
> From the right and the left, from behind and before,
> From within and without, from above and below;
> And all at once to the bishop they go.

> "They have whetted their teeth against the stones,
> And now they pick the bishop's bones:
> They gnawed the flesh from every limb;
> For they were sent to do judgment on him."

At the union of the Rhine and one of its smaller tributaries, lies a town which the lines of a poetess have made more widely known than almost any other on the river, — "Fair Bingen on the Rhine." Doubtless the lady's sketch was imaginary, and the village which she

THE "MOUSE TOWER."

thus immortalized was probably chosen at random; nevertheless, it is impossible to look upon it without a pitying thought of the "soldier of the legion," who "lay dying in Algiers"; and as the boat glides by it in its course, one finds himself repeating some of the familiar lines:

> "Tell her, the last night of my life (for ere the moon be risen,
> My body will be out of pain, my soul be out of prison),
> I dreamed I stood with her and saw the yellow sunlight shine
> On the vine-clad hills of Bingen — fair Bingen on the Rhine."

BINGEN.

Just opposite Bingen the glasses of all tourists on the steamer are eagerly turned toward the German National Monument, which stands at a height of seven hundred and forty feet above the river, on the brow of a wooded hill known as the Niederwald. It is a colossal bronze statue of Germania, designed to keep alive the fires of patriotism by commemorating the German victories in the Franco-Prussian War, which laid the foundation of the present empire. Aside from the impressive memories that it awakens, it is an imposing work of art, for the entire monument is more than one hundred feet in height, — the majestic figure of Germania, holding a crown and sword adorned with laurel wreaths, being itself thirty-three feet high. Around the pedestal are the portraits of Emperor William and the principal princes and generals of Germany, as well as fine reliefs portraying scenes in the campaign; and on the side facing the river, the sculptures represent the "Watch on the Rhine,"

THE NATIONAL MONUMENT.

the words of the noble song being appropriately inscribed beneath.

The Rhine, in its capricious windings, gives forth its treasures, one after the other, each awakening new delight. Among the pretty villages thus revealed is Bacharach, the most conspicuous feature of which is a ruin known as St. Werner's

BACHARACH.

Chapel. The origin of this building was peculiar. Saint Werner, it appears, was a young boy, who, four centuries and a half ago, was murdered by the Jews at Oberwesel. His body was flung into the river, but, instead of floating down the stream, it came miraculously up the current for some miles, and was finally washed ashore at Bacharach, scaring the murderers into confession. After such an aquatic exploit the young man was declared a saint, and the inhabitants of the town could do no less than build for him the pretty chapel, the ruins of which still grace the borders of the Rhine.

The town of Bacharach has, also, an eventful history. Some eighteen hundred years ago a Roman settlement was estab-

ST. WERNER'S CHAPEL.

lished here, and, very early becoming famous for the wine
which it produced, it was called *Ara Bacchi*, of the Altar of
Bacchus.   Even to-day an altar to the god of wine might well
be erected at Bacharach; for, on sipping the golden produce
of its vineyards, we seem to taste in every drop a ray of im-
prisoned sunshine, and recollect the German proverb which
declares :

> " At Würzburg on the Stein,
> At Hochheim on the Main,
> And Bacharach on the Rhine,
> You find the best of wine."

Not far from the town, one sees before him, in the middle
of the river, a singularly shaped structure, which certainly can
lay no claim to beauty.   It has a most inhospitable air, since
its entrance is six feet above the rock on which the building
stands, and even this is reached only by a ladder.   More than
six hundred years ago, this structure served as a convenient
toll-house, which no boats were allowed to pass without paying

AN ANCIENT TOLL HOUSE.

CASTLE OF SCHÖNBERG.

tribute, and that it was also used as a prison is evident from the fact that dungeons still exist beneath it, below the level of the river. It was even capable of sustaining a siege, being supplied with water from a well dug deeper than the bed of the surrounding stream.

All the legends of the Rhine are by no means pathetic. Thus, it is claimed that in the castle of Schönberg there once lived seven handsome daughters, who were such incorrigible flirts, and persistently broke so many hearts, that Providence finally interfered to avenge the Romeos of the Rhine, and changed the sisters into seven rocks, which stand here to

"SENSELESS STONE."

this day, a warning to all pretty voyagers of the consequences of such cruel actions.

> " Of love they ever made a jest,
> For a stony heart was in each breast;
> Now, sunk in the Rhine for their sins to atone,
> They are changed into rock and senseless stone."

The present generation, however, apparently cares very little for this warning. Providence seems to have changed its method of protecting jilted lovers; else would the shores of Mount Desert and Narragansett Pier be quite impassable for boats.

At one point on the river, German students love to perpetrate a standard joke, at which all travelers have laughed for twenty years, but which still causes merriment. The echo here from either bank is so exceptionally fine, that students often shout the question, "What is the Mayor of Oberwesel?" The echoed answer comes back from the hills, "*Esel*," that is to say, "an ass."

ST. GOAR.

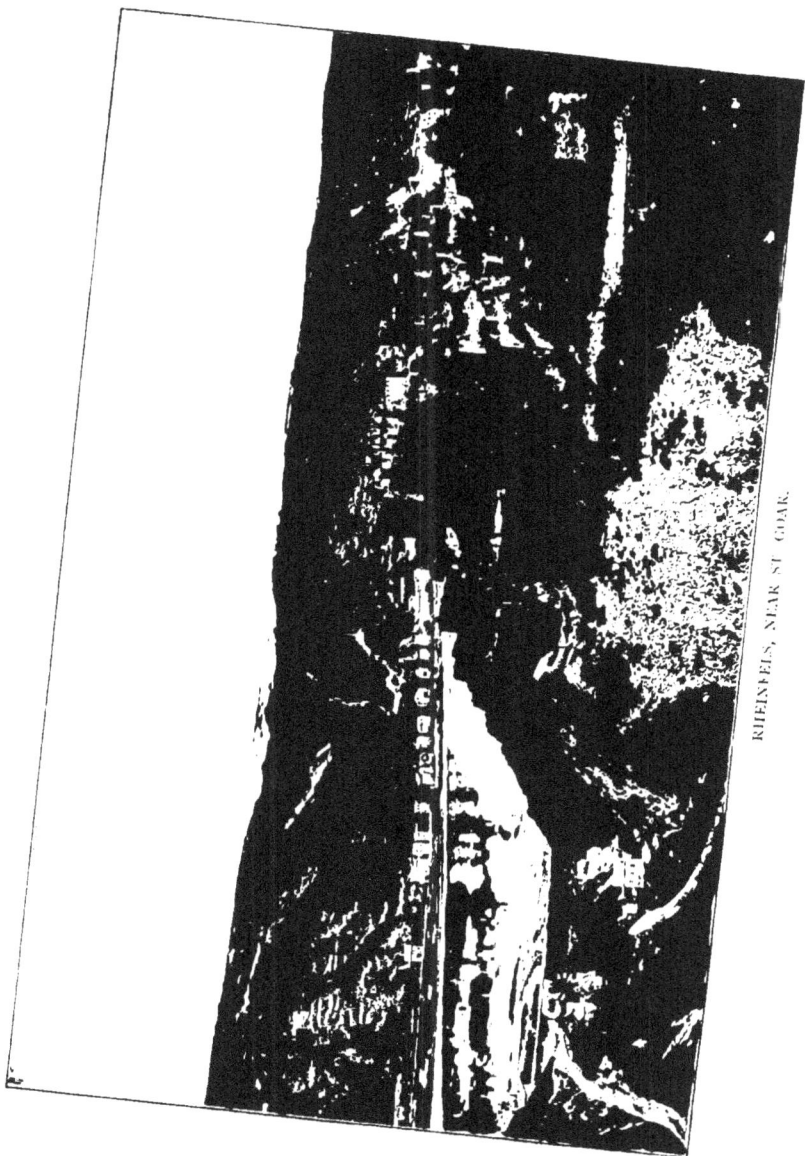

RHEINFELS, NEAR ST GOAR.

THE LORELEI.

The Rhenish village of St. Goar derives its name from an old saint of the most remarkable character and habits, who flourished here eight hundred years ago. Professionally he was a boatman, and ferried people back and forth across the Rhine; but not content with this, he sought to convert the heathen of this region to Christianity. His methods, however, were peculiar. One day, for example, as he was rowing a traveler across the Rhine, an idea suddenly came to him like an inspiration. Ceasing to row, he asked his passenger if he were a Christian. The man replied that he was not. Whereupon St. Goar immediately rushed upon him, plunged him over the side, and baptized him, ere the astonished man had time to catch his breath. Then, for fear that such a quick conversion might not last, he left him in the Rhine to drown, so that he might go at once to Paradise. The legend adds that, the same night the soul of the drowned man appeared to St. Goar, and, far from reproving him for his rough treatment, thanked him for thus securing to him the joys of Heaven. Thenceforth

THE SIREN'S CLIFF.

the valiant saint doubted no more that baptizing was his vocation, and hardly a day passed without an immersion. It is true, the bishop of the town reproved him for his undue violence, but the saint immediately wrought a miracle by hanging his hat on a sunbeam, and the bishop could not say a word. Nevertheless, this system of compulsory baptism lasted only a short time; for, naturally enough, as soon as his habits became known, each passenger, when in the middle of the stream, would always make the sign of the cross, and swear with chattering teeth that he was a Christian.

At a little distance below St. Goar, the finest scenery on the Rhine reveals itself, where the imposing cliffs of the Lorelei rise, dark and threatening, to the height of four hundred and fifty feet. Combined with beauty here, there used to be, in the days of small boats, dependent merely upon oar and sail, an element of danger. For at this point the Rhine is sometimes turbulent, and in a distance of one hundred yards the inclination of the river-bed is about five feet. Even now, a sunken ledge still makes a whirlpool, dangerous to small craft, unless skillfully managed. The curious legend of the place is, therefore, easily explained; for, in the evening, when the white foam beat against the rocks, and the pale moonbeams rested phantom-like on the frowning cliffs, the peasants fancied they perceived the golden hair and ivory shoulders of a siren who lured poor mariners to their destruction. But now, at all events, the Lorelei has lost her power. A railroad tunnel perforates the rock, the steamboat's whistle drowns the melody of her voice, and she spreads the meshes of her whirlpool-net in vain.

Not far below this siren-haunted cliff, I visited one day two famous ruins, standing side by side, called the Castles of the Brothers. The picture of the Rhine, seen through the crumbling arches, was enchanting, but the old walls were gaunt and bare as skeletons, and their deserted windows called to mind the eyeless sockets of a skull. Their legend is well suited to the place; for, it is said, two brothers once resided here in perfect harmony, until a fatal shadow crossed their path in the form of a mad, unconquerable passion for the same woman. In such a love, appeals to generosity are useless. Neither brother would yield his claim; and upon a narrow ledge between the castles they finally met in mortal combat.

THE CASTLES OF THE BROTHERS.

FALKENBURG.

At the same instant, the sword of his opponent pierced each lover's breast, and the two brothers fell in death, a look of hatred, yet of triumph, on each face.

The massive walls of Falkenburg commemorate a famous bandit of the Rhine, named Falkenstein, who on one occasion looked with envious eyes upon the silver bell of a church, and caused it to be brought to him that he might melt it into coin. The bishop, struck with horror at the sacrilege, went to the castle in his priestly robes to demand its return. At this, Falkenstein burst into a roar of laughter, saying: "You wish to have your bell, do you? Well, you shall have it henceforth forever." Thereupon the bell was tied about the bishop's neck, and both were thrown into the dungeon-well of the tower, and covered with stones to the

THE JUNCTION OF THE RHINE AND MOSEL.

depth of six feet. A few days afterward Falkenstein fell ill,
and when night came, the doctor and astrologer who watched
beside his bed heard with terror the knell of the silver bell
coming from the depths of the earth. The awful sound continued until midnight, when, at the last stroke of twelve,
Falkenstein expired. Since then, as regularly as the anni-
versary of the desperado's death comes round, it is said the bell
can be heard ringing under the ruined castle.

Not far from this point, we approach the confluence of
the Rhine and the Mosel, the water of which is as pleasing
to the sight, as is to the taste the sparkling Mosel wine produced along its banks. This river, even after uniting with
the Rhine, preserves for a long time its emerald color, as
though unwilling to mingle its French waters with the waves
of Germany. The city of Coblentz which is situated at the
union of these streams has an interesting history. Here,
eighteen hundred years ago, the Romans founded a city
named appropriately Confluentes; and hither, after the death

EHRENBREITSTEIN.

of Charlemagne, his grandsons came to divide between them his gigantic empire. In a military point of view Coblentz is of great importance, and hence is thoroughly protected, not only by its own massive walls and a connected series of strong forts, but also by the mighty citadel of Ehrenbreitstein, just across the Rhine. This stone colossus is defended by four hundred cannon, and is said to contain fifty thousand needle-guns, and stores of provisions capable of maintaining an army of eight thousand men for ten years, while it derives

THE PROMENADE AT COBLENTZ.

its water from deep wells dug within its own enclosure. Its very name, the Broadstone of Honor, is imposing; and, rising as it does in massive majesty four hundred feet above the river, it seems sufficiently impregnable to deserve the appellation sometimes given it of the "Gibraltar of the Rhine."

The most beautiful feature of Coblentz is the Rhine Promenade, which borders the historic stream for more than two miles. I hardly know a prettier walk in Europe than this river-avenue; for, aside from its charming situation, it is a thing of art and beauty. Far from being a mere promenade, as the name might imply, it is a lovely garden, sloping to the Rhine, kept with the utmost care, shaded by noble trees, carpeted with turf, embellished with statues, fountains,

EHRENBREITSTEIN CASTLE.

and elaborate flower-beds, and frequently enlivened with choice
music. This river-park was designed by the Empress Augusta,
who was exceedingly fond of Coblentz, and to her memory
a statue has been erected here, which seems to be contemplating with serene satisfaction the scene of beauty called
by her into existence.

One evening, as I was strolling on this promenade, watching the stars reflected in the river, and reveling in the peaceful beauty of the place, I suddenly heard in the distance the
harmonious voices of some German students singing "The
Watch on the Rhine." It was beautifully sung, and I stood
spell-bound, listening to the thrilling words which rang out
with true manly vigor over the historic stream. I was not,
it is true, a German, and hence could not perhaps entirely
appreciate the pride and joy therein expressed; but even as a
stranger from beyond the sea, I felt the blood stir quickly
in my veins, as those rich voices sang beneath the stars:

"While yet one drop of life-blood flows,
The sword shall never know repose;
While yet one arm the shot can pour,
The foe shall never reach thy shore.
Rest, Fatherland, for sons of thine
Shall steadfast keep the Wacht am Rhein."

COBLENTZ.

STOLZENFELS.

The castle of Stolzenfels, or Proud Rock, which is set in a frame of foliage, four hundred feet above the river, looks sometimes from the steamer like a castle floating in the air. This picturesque château is said to have been in existence for a thousand years, and we can well believe that such a site could hardly fail to be improved at the earliest opportunity. Even in its present restoration, the old foundation walls were used, and its original form was preserved as far as possible.

Like the Rheinstein, the castle of Stolzenfels is now the property of Emperor William; and here his grandmother, the Empress Augusta, loved to spend a considerable portion of her time. Her choice is easily

THE TERRACE AT STOLZENFELS.

comprehended; for what more enchanting home could be desired than this, in which to pass some weeks or months in calm retirement? The isolation need not be so great as one would at first suppose; for cities are within easy distance, the railway and the river lie below, while telephone and telegraph wires convey to it, at lightning speed, the news and gossip of the world. Yet, if one wishes it,

THE KNIGHTS' HALL.

here is perfect quiet. A lovely forest offers shaded walks, the air is always fresh and cool, and the magnifi-

A ROOM IN STOLZENFELS.

cent prospect of the Rhine, stretching away for miles to north and south, surpasses the power of language to describe. When traveling in Switzerland, Greece, Italy, or the Rhineland, I have never failed to have with me for immediate reference a little volume of "Childe Harold"; and it was while looking down upon the Rhine from the terrace of

Stolzenfels, one summer afternoon, that I appreciated as never
before the lines of Byron:

> " The river nobly foams and flows,
> The charm of this enchanted ground,
> And all its thousand turns disclose
> Some fresher beauty varying round ;
> The haughtiest breast its wish might bound
> Through life to dwell delightful here ;
> Nor could on earth a spot be found
> To nature and to me so dear.
> Could thy dear eyes in following mine
> Still sweeten more these banks of Rhine."

Almost directly opposite this castle is the river Lahn,
another tributary of the Rhine, upon whose banks, in a
charming little
valley, is the town
of Ems, a pretty
watering place,
which enjoys a
world-wide repu-
tation. Upon the
summit of a hill
which overlooks
the town, the
Germans have
erected a national
monument, sur-
mounted by an
eagle; for Ems
is closely asso-
ciated with the nation's history. Not only was it for years
a favorite resort of the old Emperor William, but, in 1870,
it became the scene of an important political event. It
was here that the famous interview occurred between the
German Emperor and the French ambassador Benedetti,

STOLZENFELS AND THE RIVER LAHN.

CAPELLEN AND STOLZENFELS.

in which the Kaiser's manner was construed as an affront to the French nation. It was the one thing wanting to precipitate the impending conflict. France instantly declared the war which was to prove so fatal to her; and thus the spark, ignited here at Ems, soon set all Europe in a blaze, and caused Napoleon III. to be, within six months, a prisoner at Cassel, and the Kaiser a conqueror at Versailles. Many stories of the old Emperor's life at Ems are recounted, one of which states that on a certain occasion he paid a visit to an orphan asylum in the neighborhood, and, calling one

THE NATIONAL MONUMENT, EMS.

of the little girls, began to question her. "My little fräulein," he began, taking an orange from his pocket, "can you tell me to what kingdom this belongs?" "To the vegetable kingdom," she replied. "Very good," said the Kaiser. Then, holding up a gold piece, he inquired, "And to what kingdom does this belong?" "To the mineral kingdom," she answered promptly. "Well done!" exclaimed the Emperor. "But now," he added, "to what kingdom do I belong?" The child hesitated. She could not say that her revered Emperor belonged to the animal kingdom. Accordingly she answered timidly: "Your Majesty belongs to the kingdom of Heaven!" The old Kaiser smiled, but there were tears in his eyes, as he replied, "My little one, I hope that you are right."

The visitor to Ems, a score of years ago, would often meet, in one of the hotels or on the promenade, a thin-faced, wrinkled man, who was none other than the hero of the Franco-Prussian War, Von Moltke, commander-in-chief of the German army. Unlike the Emperor and Prince Bismarck, he used to travel with extreme simplicity, and unannounced, for he disliked receptions and publicity, and was content with the plainest rooms. His traveling experiences were, therefore, sometimes amusing. One afternoon he entered a hotel at Ems, his satchel in his hand, having preferred to walk the little distance from the station. He wore the dress of a civilian, and looked decidedly travel-worn and dusty. Accordingly, the landlord told the waiter to show the old man to a small room under the eaves. Once there, the waiter produced the usual card, and asked the stranger to inscribe his name and residence. What was the landlord's horror, when he read the words, "Field Marshal Von Moltke, Berlin"! "*Ach, mein Gott!* what have I done?" exclaimed the wretched man, wringing his hands. "I am ruined!" Rushing upstairs, he begged the marshal to descend. "It is all a mistake," he cried, "a terrible mistake,

GENERAL VIEW OF EMS.

I have beautiful rooms for your excellency on the first floor."
"What is the price of them?" asked Von Moltke. "Only
one hundred francs a day, your excellency." "And the
price of this room?"   "Oh, a mere trifle, three francs a day."
"Then I will stay," replied the marshal, "I am quite comfortable here; and
many a time upon
the battle-field, I
should have been
very glad of such
a bed as this."

Crowning an
eminence, not far

THE KING'S SEAT.

from Stolzenfels,
is a little struc-
ture called the
Königsstuhl, or
King's Seat, not
as one might sup-
pose, because
some sovereign

THE COVERED GALLERY AT EMS.

ever used it as a post of observation, but from the fact that it
has actually played an important part in royal history. Five
hundred years ago, it was erected by the Emperor Charles IV.,
and even now, although rebuilt in 1843, still keeps its ancient
form, and is in part composed of the original stones which have

THE SEVEN MOUNTAINS AND NONNENWERTH.

successfully with-
stood the storms of
centuries. It looked
to me as I ap-
proached it like a
roofless chapel, but in reality is an octagonal platform surrounded
by seven arches, and supporting seven stone seats on which the
princes sat whose privilege it was to choose the Emperor of
Germany. Here, then, under the open sky, and overlooking the
majestic stream which mirrored it, the seven Electors of the
empire used to meet, not only to select their sovereign, but to
make laws, issue proclamations, and conclude treaties with foreign nations. It gives one a curious sensation to look upon
this simple "seat" and realize how much power was once vested
in the men who met here to exalt or dethrone kings. They
were in fact the "power behind the throne" and entitled to all
royal dignities and honors save the title of majesty. Were they
not wise to thus secure the substance and let the shadow go?

The most conspicuous elevations near the Rhine are
known as the Seven Mountains. The loftiest of these is

ANDERNACH.

the historic Drachenfels, or Dragon's Rock, named from that
legendary monster of the Rhine which, in the days when
Roman legions came this way, was both the scourge and
terror of the region. The memory of this dragon has not
been forgotten ; for the evil which beasts do, sometimes, lives
after them, while "the good is oft interred with their bones."
At all events, the castle on this height perpetuates its story,
and the red wine which comes from the mountain-side is
called by the un-
appetizing title
of the "Dragon's
blood."

The legend of
the hero, Sieg-
fried, who slew
the monster, and
became invulner-
able by bathing in
its blood, has been
immortalized in
song and story.
Another myth,
however, makes
the slayer of the
dragon a woman.

THE DRACHENFELS.

According to this tradition, the savage beast used to descend
the mountain every day, like a roaring lion seeking whom he
might devour. The Romans, however, resolved to change its
mode of life and make it more domestic in its habits. They,
therefore, adopted the custom of bringing daily to the dragon's
cave some prisoner whom they had seized. One day, among
the captives, was a girl so beautiful that two centurions were on
the point of fighting a duel to see which of them should claim
her as his own, when the Roman general interfered, and said

that for the sake of peace, the maiden should be given
to neither of them, but should be handed over to the
dragon.   This decision was much admired in the army, and
was by some compared to the judgment of Solomon.   The
next day, therefore, the victim was led to the dragon's cave.
The monster soon appeared.   For some time it had been
suffering from dyspepsia.   The Romans had not always been
careful to remove
the sandals from
the feet of their
captives, and
these had been
as hard for the
dragon to digest
as railway sand-
wiches are for us.
At the sight,
therefore, of this
lovely morsel, the
dragon   howled
for joy, and ad-
vanced,   smack-
ing its lips and

THE ASCENT OF THE DRACHENFELS.

rattling its scales like a thousand tambourines.   But the
young maiden was a Christian, and in the pocket of her
polonaise, or whatever article of clothing corresponded to
it, she had a crucifix.   This she drew forth and displayed to the advancing dragon.   At sight of it the huge
beast stood for a moment petrified with horror; then, with
a roar that made the mountain tremble, it fell back down
the cliffs, and was dashed to pieces on the rocks below.
Whichever legend we adopt as true, certain it is that the
only monster on the Drachenfels to-day is the iron horse,
which, though occasionally emitting fire and smoke, is, never-

theless, completely tamed, and in the summer season meekly draws a party of tourists to the summit eighteen times a day. The ancient castle, built more than seven hundred years ago, is now a melancholy ruin, but, since 1883, the mountain has been crowned by a magnificent edifice called the Drachenburg, which is the property of a wealthy German baron.

The view from the summit of the Drachenfels is glorious. The river lies like an avenue of silver, between two limitless

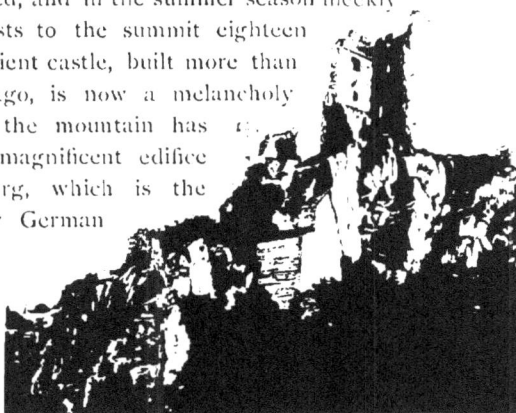

THE RUINED CASTLE OF THE DRACHENFELS.

expanses of variously colored cultivated fields, traversed by lines of tiny roads resembling wires on a vase of cloisonné, and dotted here and there with white-walled buildings, which in the distance look like children's playthings scattered on a

DRACHENFELS.

Persian rug. I know of nothing comparable to the impression gained by looking down from a great height upon a thickly settled plain. If one can only be alone at such a time, and have an opportunity to think quietly, he can easily imagine himself contemplating the world from another sphere, and hence can fancy how our earth must look to those removed from all its sordid cares and petty intrigues. For, at that elevation, the towns have dwindled into ant-hills, and human beings rushing to and fro in them, if visible at all, appear like insects; and their ambitions, quarrels, loves, and hates seem hardly more important than the vibrations of a gnat's wings, compared with the sublime ideas of Time and Space, Creation and Eternity, which meet him face to face upon the heights, and show him all that he has lost by lingering so long below.

On the opposite bank of the river from the Drachenfels, and at an elevation of three hundred and fifty feet above the Rhine, stands the ruined tower of Rolandseck, the view from which is almost unsurpassed. Of all the ruins on the river

VIEW FROM THE DRACHENFELS.

this has, perhaps, the most poetic legend; for it is said to have been built by the brave and handsome Roland, the nephew of Charlemagne. According to one of several stories, he was betrothed to the daughter of the Lord of Drachenfels, the

A GLIMPSE FROM ROLANDSECK.

fairest maiden on the Rhine, and they had pledged themselves before God, either to wed each other, or to renounce the world. But ere the nuptials could be celebrated, Roland was summoned by Charlemagne to the war against the Moors. There he accomplished prodigies of valor, and, finally, in the battle of the Pyrénées, was grievously wounded and reported dead. Hearing this news, the broken-hearted maiden, faithful to her vow, entered a convent. One night, however, having regained his health and strength, Roland returned, eager to claim

RUINS OF ROLANDSECK

his bride. To his amazement he was told that she was an inmate of a convent on the neighboring island of Nonnenwerth. On hearing this, Roland himself renounced the world, and building a hermitage, lived in full view of the convent for several years. Only once in that time did he see the face of his beloved; and that was when the sisters of the cloister brought her forth for burial. Thenceforth the unhappy prince refused all food, and died with his last glance turned toward the island which thus in life and death had claimed from him his bride.

THE RHINE AND NONNENWERTH.

Upon this island a convent, embowered in trees, still occupies the site of the institution founded centuries ago, and it is said that this historic retreat was conceded to the nuns by Napoleon, through the intercession of Josephine, at the time when all other religious establishments along the Rhine were abolished by the French.

We may smile at the old Rhenish legends as improbable and childish, and yet to the ideas which underlie them the world owes some of those immortal compositions which must no longer be regarded as the "music of the future," but the music of the century. Wagner perceived the strength and beauty of the northern myths and drew from them material for his noblest inspirations. Then, bringing to the Rhine the

LAHNECH, OBERLAHNSTEIN.

legendary heroes of the North, he wove about them the enchanting robes of music, poetry, and romance.

The Rhine itself with its eternal movement toward the sea, the changeless calm within its depths, the rhythmic undulation of its surface, the whisper of its wavelets in the rushes, the clamor of its current on the rocks, and the wild fury of its falls, furnished the motive for some of his sublimest passages.

There is, indeed, a power in the Norseland Sagas that makes them masterful and virile; and such conceptions as the Rheingold, the valiant Siegfried, the weird Valkyrie, and the Twilight of the Gods, are better suited to Wagner's music than the more effeminate mythology of the south could ever be. The Valhalla, not Olympus, is Wagnerian.

THE ISLAND OF NONNENWERTH.

In full view of the Seven Mountains lies the pretty city of Bonn, famed for its university of fifteen hundred students. It is a pleasant place in which to spend a few days of the fortnight or three weeks which can be profitably given to a tour in Rhineland; for its hotels are excellent, the surrounding scenery charming, and the excursions to be made from it delightful. Among the celebrated names associated with Bonn are those of the historian Niebuhr and the philosopher Schlegel,

who taught in its university; the composer Beethoven, whose
birthplace it was; and the poet Arndt, whose noble life here
reached its end.   To the composer and poet, monuments have
been erected, and as I stood before them and reflected on the
rarity of men who rise thus from the wilderness of mediocrity,
and are thenceforth distinguished evermore from the innumerable nameless dead, I was profoundly convinced of the potency
and value of *individuality* in human history.   It was Socrates,
not the Athenians, who gave mankind the ideas handed down
to us by his disciples Xenophon and Plato; it was Cæsar, not
the Roman legions, who conquered Gaul, invaded Britain,
vanquished Pompey, and unified the Roman world; it was
Frederick the Great, not the Prussian army, who kept at bay
the three great European powers for seven years; it was
Napoleon, not his marshals, nor even the spirit of the Revolution, who entered nearly every capital as conqueror, created
kings, and was the arbiter of Europe for a dozen years.   The

BONN

masses of humanity are like the steppes or prairies of our earth, — extensive, useful, and productive, but painfully monotonous and uniform. The leaders of the race, however, are like mountains which lift their heads toward heaven, discern the future and survey the past, hold converse with each other over the intervening fields and foothills, catch the first promise of the rising sun, reflect it to a darkened world beneath, and finally pass on the solar radiance to more distant peaks, till their refulgent

STATUE OF BEETHOVEN.

summits seem like a line of torch-bearers encircling the globe.

It is difficult to think of either Shakespeare or Beethoven as a child, and yet the man whose influence in music has been as helpful and inspiring to the race as Shakespeare was in literature, played as a boy in these old streets of Bonn.

Equally remarkable in another way was the poet Arndt, the inspired bard of Germany during the great uprising of the nation against Napoleon. His patriotic songs were then to German hearts what military music is to weary limbs, and his immortal lyric: "What is the German Fatherland?" — "Was ist des Deutschen Vaterland?" — is still almost as popular in Germany as the "Watch on the Rhine." At a time when from all parts of Germany recruits were hurrying to the front, with the one purpose of liberating their country from the oppression it had borne so long, the following lines were sung upon the march or round their camp-fires, and awakened wonderful enthusiasm and fraternal feeling:

"What is the German's Fatherland?
The Prussian land? the Swabian land?
Where Rhine's thick-clustering fruitage gleams?
Where on the Belt the sea-mew screams?
     Not these the land;
     His is a wider Fatherland.

What is the German's Fatherland?
Bavarian, or Westphalian land?
Where on the Dunes the wild sand blows?
Or where the Danube brawling flows?
     Not these the land;
     His is a wider Fatherland.

What is the German's Fatherland?
Oh, name at length this mighty land!
As wide as sounds the German tongue,
And German hymns to God are sung,
     That is, the land;
     That, German, name thy Fatherland.

To us this glorious land is given;
O Lord of Hosts, look down from heaven,
And grant us German loyalty,
To love our country faithfully;
     To love our land,
     Our undivided Fatherland."

STATUE OF ARNDT.

Besides his patriotic songs, Arndt also wrote some pamphlets — notably the "Spirit of the Age" and a "Cate-

COLOGNE.

chism for Germany's Defenders " — whereby he appealed
directly to the purest impulses and noblest sentiments of his
countrymen.   It is fitting, therefore, that he should have
lived, revered and beloved by every one, to the extreme age
of ninety years, "a marvel of vitality, faith, and heartiness,
— a wonderful old man." His house in Bonn was near the
Rhine, and overlooked the river at perhaps the most beauti-
ful portion of its course. | On a stone bench by his door
old "Father Arndt," as | he was called, would sit for
hours, gazing upon the   Rhine, and musing on the
national changes   and improvements he had

GODESBURG CASTLE.

seen and helped to bring about ;
and when he died, in 1860, an
immense multitude of people followed his body to the grave.
He had already marked the place where he desired to be
buried, under an oak tree planted by his own hands; and
there, before the grave was closed, one of his own inspiring
hymns was sung, and, as the music of its closing words

THE RHINE, NEAR ROLANDSECK.

floated away to lose itself above the Rhine, the precious dust of the old patriot was given to the embrace of his beloved Fatherland, which will forever guard it faithfully under the cross of stone which bears his name.

Of all the cities that adorn the splendid panorama of the Rhine, Cologne is both the wealthiest and most renowned. It played a prominent part even in Roman history, and during the Middle Ages was occasionally called the "Rome of the North." Here Trajan received the summons to assume the imperial purple; here Vitellius and Silvanus were proclaimed emperors; and here the latter was murdered by his cohorts. Here, also, in the camp of Germanicus,

VIEW OF COLOGNE.

Agrippina, the mother of Nero, was born, who, in A.D.
51, retaining an affection for her birthplace, established a
colony of Roman veterans, to which she gave her name,
Colonia Agrippina, — whence the modern name Cologne.

Numerous churches greet the eye as one surveys this
city from the Rhine, but its dominant feature is, of course,
its glorious cathedral. Those who beheld this building
twenty years ago would hardly recognize it now. Then, it
resembled the
hull of a huge ship
without masts,
since its great
towers lacked
completion. For
centuries it had
remained unfin-
ished, — a splen-
did promise made
to God, but unful-
filled. During
six hundred and
thirty-two years
the mighty monu-
ment had grown,

THE CATHEDRAL.

little by little; now halting for a generation, now actually
retrograding, and very narrowly escaping ruin. Begun in
1248, it was not finished till 1880, when the last stone
was finally placed in position; and the completion of the
edifice was celebrated in the presence of old Emperor
William and nearly all the princes of Germany. At
present it has a glory and a majesty that lift it heavenward above all other churches in the world, and make of
it a vast stone arch, bridging the stream of time, down which
the intervening years have swept on to eternity. It is im-

THE TOWERS.

possible to gaze on either the exterior or interior of the stupendous edifice without feeling well-nigh crushed by an overpowering realization of the sublime. The spires reach the almost unexampled height of five hundred and twelve feet, which is just equal to the entire length of the cathedral; and the height of the gable in the transept exactly corresponds to the cathedral's width. It is, therefore, the most regular and stupendous Gothic structure in existence, the consummation of grandeur and religion. When one stands at night beside its base, and lets his gaze climb slowly upward over its enormous buttresses and towers, the effect is mountainous, and its architecture appears Alpine in sublimity, the mighty shafts (which seem as solid as the eternal hills yet are as graceful as the elm) rising until their summits vanish in the gloom, like a colossal stairway leading up to heaven. At such a time, when we consider all the numberless details of the vast edifice, in flying-buttresses, statues, gargoyles, turrets, foliage, and fretwork, — each perfect and complete, and wrought in centuries past by men who did their little part, and then passed on, yielding their place to others, — the grand cathedral seems a fitting emblem of the progress of our race, and the lesson which it teaches may be thus interpreted:

"Life is a leaf of paper white,
  Whereon each one of us may write
  His word or two, and then comes night.
  Greatly begin! though thou have time
  But for a line, be that sublime, —
  Not failure, but low aim, is crime."

Moreover, the history of this building is as full of interest as its grand framework is of majesty. The hands of cunning artisans were fashioning its walls two hundred and fifty years before Columbus sailed for the New World. It antedates by fifty years the founding of the Turkish Empire. Kingdoms have risen and fallen, cities and dynasties have flourished and have passed away since the original architect of this cathedral saw its first stone lowered into the place where it has slumbered all these years. And now that the great work is done, and the cross gleams upon its loftiest pinnacle, how sad it seems that its creator's name should be unknown! For it is his

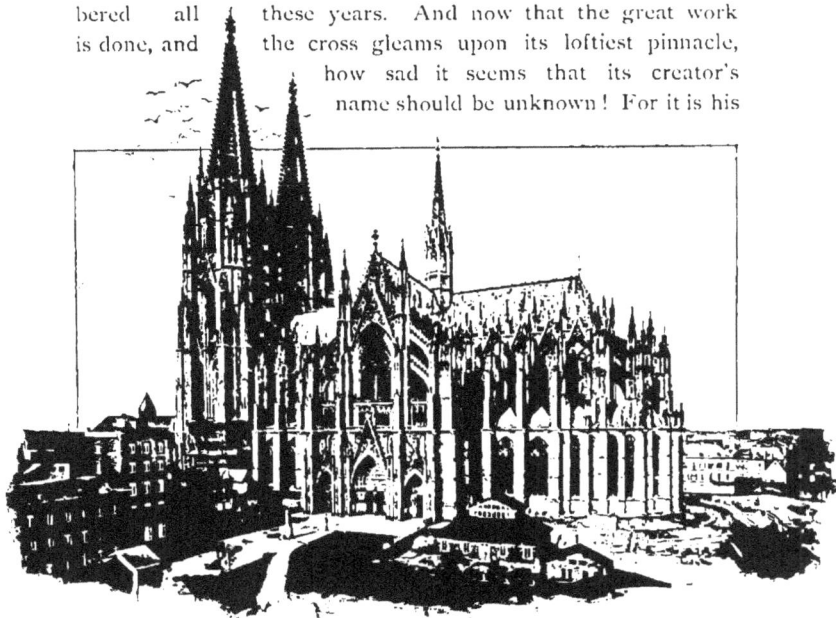

THE GLORY OF COLOGNE.

THE INTERIOR OF COLOGNE CATHEDRAL.

design that has thus triumphed over time and all inferior sug-
gestions for six hundred years. This fact has been accounted
for by a legend, which states that the architect was one night
walking on the river's bank, despairing of ever achieving his
ideal, when Satan suddenly appeared to him and offered him
the most magnificent plan, if he would give him in exchange
his soul. "Will my name become famous?" asked the artist.
"It will forever rank with that of Phidias," was the reply.
The architect begged for a night in which to consider the
matter, and consulted a cunning priest, who advised him
to take the devil's plan for a moment in his hands, and,
while conversing, to glance at it and master its details. The
artist did so, and then declined to make the bargain. Whereupon Satan, seeing himself outwitted, cried: "You have broken
faith with me. So be it. Only remember this, and let it haunt
your dying hour, that when this temple shall have been com-

pleted after my design, and the whole world is ringing with
its praises, your name will be entirely unknown." Whatever
we may think of the legend, the architect's reward has certainly been oblivion.

Beyond Cologne, the Rhine sweeps onward like a king
whose fame and power are secure. Its life-work is well-
nigh accomplished. It has apparently received from the
uplifted towers of the old cathedral its absolution and its
benediction. What a career it has had since we first beheld
it, leaving its cradle in the glacier, clearing Schaffhausen's
barrier at a bound, or gliding by the castles on its banks!
Once more it calls to mind a human life, but now, a life the
sands of which are running low, and whose long drama has-
tens to completion; for, at its terminus,
silently awaiting its inevi-
table com- ing, is
the open sea.

"THE OPEN SEA."

Disraeli said that life consists of three parts: youth, a delusion; manhood, a struggle; old age, a regret. How true this
is of the delusion and the struggle, we all know; but few
regrets can sadden a career which, like the noble river we
have followed, leaves, after years of progress and beneficence,
its finished duties and confining shores for the unbounded
ocean of a higher destiny.

BELGIUM

BELGIUM

T HE supreme benefit of travel lies in the priceless recollections which we bring back from our wanderings. Memory is the key that, in our hours of revery, unlocks hall after hall of happy reminiscences whose number and variety are limited only by the tours we have made. Travel enables us to make the conquest of the world, appreciative observation garners up its harvest, and memory furnishes the feast. The only joys of which we are sure are those of memory. Behind the pleasure of the present lurks the fear of loss; before anticipated happiness lies the dread of disappointment; but joys we have experienced remain in memory beyond the possibility of change.

KING LEOPOLD.

Many experiences in the traveler's life are more enjoyable in retrospect than in reality. Bad weather, illness, accidents, or uncongenial company may sadly mar our happiness in picture-gallery and cathedral, or on

IN THE PARK, BRUSSELS.

lake and mountain-pass ; but when, in the leisure of life's autumn, we mentally survey the fields of travel, we find that while the wings of time have scattered the chaff, judgment has winnowed and memory has preserved all that was precious in the golden grain.

A tourist may return from travel penniless, yet be a mental millionaire; while some illiterate Cræsus, who has never visited the shrines of Nature, Art, and History is, in the realm of memory, a bankrupt. For the enthusiastic traveler a word, a sound, a perfume, or a picture may, like the fabled touch of Midas, transmute the most prosaic substance into gold. Oh, the joy of it! To have a simple strain of music bring before us moonlit evenings on the Grand Canal, a roseate cloud recall the Alpen-glow upon Mont Blanc, a passing Japanese remind us of the sacred grove of Nikko, the rhythm of a waltz transport us to the Danube, the tawny sand within an hour-glass hint of the Sahara, and the rich fragrance of a Jacqueminot suggest the rose garden where blooms in fadeless beauty that perfect flower of architecture, — the Taj Mahal.

For those whose memories cannot be awakened thus, Art furnishes the more direct suggestion of the photograph. The

sun has now become man's slave, and through its subtile
agency the wonders of the world are printed with infallible
accuracy, and multiplied so easily that the humblest village
of a civilized country possesses sun-etched reproductions of
fine scenery and works of art, just as a wayside pool may
hold within its shallow breast the beautiful re-
flection of a cloudless sky.

The benefits of travel —
who can doubt
them? It were
as foolish to deny
the good results
of reading. What
is the whole world
but an open book,
whose author is
Almighty God, and
on the pages of
which have been
written more or
less distinctly sto-
ries of the various
races of humanity?

I am pro-
foundly grateful
for the irrepres-
sible longing to
visit the Old World
that made my
childhood
one long
dream
of his-
tory and

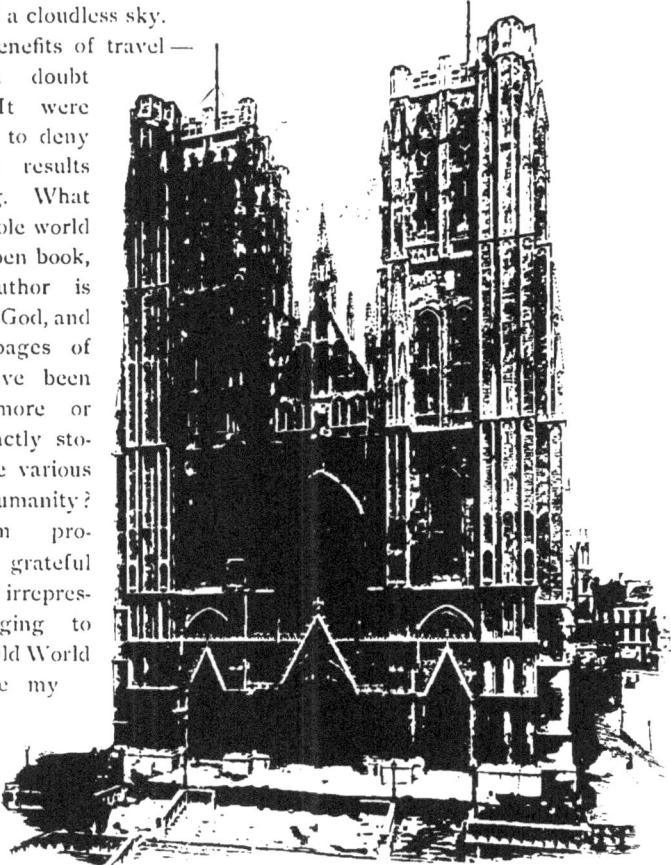

travel; for by its realization the remainder of my life will
be replete with memories which are at once a joy and an
inspiration.

At any moment, I can walk in fancy through the picture-
gallery of memory, and see countless landscapes tinted by the
suns of many lands. With
slower pulse and calmer
heart, I feel the youthful
eagerness for sight-seeing
and adventure gradually
changing into a profound
contentment, born of the
knowledge that the mental
pictures, gathered through
a score of years, cannot be
taken from me, and are destined to remain, fadeless
and indestructible while life
shall last. No vandal hand
can mar my inner vision
of the Himalayas. Saint

REMBRANDT.

Peter's dome may be destroyed by fire, but I shall see it still
in its perfection. No dust can gather on the scenes I follow
with closed eyes, as memory deftly draws the curtain of imagination and unfolds the panorama of the past. In castle or
cottage, wealth or poverty, my treasures will not leave me;
and in my easy chair I make the tour of the world upon the
wings of thought with perfect ease, floating on waters which
lave distant shores; tracing familiar mountains in the sunset clouds; kneeling in temple, church, or mosque; drifting
through tropic seas; climbing the cones of Popocatepetl and
Vesuvius; and watching either the sudden disappearance of
the sun beneath the desert sands, or its persistent brilliancy
at midnight in the Arctic sky.

Among the many scenes thus happily recalled, few are more interesting than those connected with the Netherlands. For centuries Belgium and Holland have been called the Low Countries; but their deficiency in altitude has not consigned them to obscurity. On the contrary, if valiant men, fine arts, and famous deeds are made the test of greatness, few countries in the world are so conspicuous in the light of history. Compared with the leading European nations of this century, the Netherlands are at present insignificant, and it is not improbable that they will, ultimately, be absorbed by France and Germany, which stand continually ready to appropriate them. To-day, however, "lying low" in their small, quiet corner of the Continent, they form a most attractive place of sojourn for the traveler; as, in a picture-gallery, we sometimes turn from the large halls with their bewildering display of famous paintings, to enter a charming little cabinet, where dainty miniatures, cloisonné faïence, or exquisitely finished art-studies afford a combination of rare pleasure and a sense of rest.

The Belgians evidently love their native land; for there is comparatively little emigration from it, and none of the other European countries equals Belgium in density of population (the average being about four hundred and eighty-five to the square

THE BURGOMASTER'S FOUNTAIN, BRUSSELS.

mile), while villages and cities are so thickly strewn upon
its fertile surface that Philip II. said the whole country was
only one large town. Of Holland Philip was less complimen-
tary, since he called it "the country nearest hell."

The inhabitants of Belgium are composed of two distinct
races, almost as different from each other in racial characteristics as are the Germans from the French. The northern provinces, bordering mainly on the North Sea, are inhabited by the
Flemings, a sturdy, blue-eyed, fair-haired people of Teutonic
origin, somewhat akin to
the Dutch. In fact, the
language spoken by them
closely resembles that of
Holland, and the Dutch
and Flemish read each
other's newspapers, al-
though they cannot very
well understand each
other's conversation. In
this portion of Belgium —
which constitutes the real
Flanders — are located the
interesting old cities,
Bruges and Ghent, as well
as the great seaport, Antwerp ; but, aside from the
important commercial in-

CASTLE OF THE COUNT OF FLANDERS.

terests of the latter city and the lace-making of Ghent and
Bruges, the population of these provinces is mainly engaged
in agriculture.

In southern Belgium, however, which is the manufacturing
part of the kingdom, lives an entirely different people known
as the Walloons. They are descendants of the Gauls, and are,
as a rule, of a high-strung nervous temperament, with dark com-

plexions and lively dispositions, like the French. These people
speak not only French, but a dialect of the French language,
known as the Walloon, which more closely resembles the old *pro-
vençal* of southern France than does the modern French itself.

The splendid cities and prosperous towns in these Walloon provinces of
Belgium, full of
industrial life and
enterprise, and
inhabited by
thrifty, pleasure-
loving people, are
profoundly inter-
esting and attract-
ive, and the ex-
quisite beauty and
charm of their
river valleys and
wooded hills,
dotted here and
there with a

A FLEMISH FAMILY.

stately castle, leave ineffaceable impressions on the memory.

It is strange that two such dissimilar races as the phlegmatic Flemish farmers and the light-hearted Walloon workmen
should coalesce and form a homogeneous people; yet such is
the fact. The Flemish element is the larger, constituting about
four-sevenths of the population, and is devoutly Roman Catho-
lic in religion and conservative in politics; while, on the other
hand, the Walloons are usually very liberal in their political
and religious views. Yet the two races make a happy, contented people, and meet on common ground in the beautiful
capital, Brussels, where each is represented in all branches of
the administration, as well as in the courts of justice and the
two Houses of Parliament.

Brussels, the capital of Belgium, is often called a miniature Paris. In fact, a traveler suddenly transported thither would hardly know that he was not in some retired section of the French metropolis. The same language is spoken in Brussels as in Paris; similar street signs greet us everywhere; the creamy color of the buildings is analogous to that which makes the city of the Seine so light and cheerful in appearance; the style of architecture, also, in both cities is nearly identical; and even the shops, cafés, and covered passageways in Brussels are thoroughly Parisian in appearance. Friends who have lived in this bright city of the Belgians assure me that it is far superior, as a place of residence, to many larger Continental capitals; and it is therefore singular that Englishmen and Americans who wish to spend considerable time abroad, in order to perfect themselves in the French language, almost

THE GALERIE ST. HUBERT, BRUSSELS.

invariably go to
Paris, where the
large English-
speaking colony
and the incessant
whirl of gaiety
make serious
study well-nigh
impossible.

The central
situation of Brus-
sels, also, renders
it very advanta-
geous as a place
of sojourn. Lon-
don, Paris, Berlin,
and Berne are

THE EDEN, BRUSSELS.

about equally distant from the Belgian metropolis, which
may in consequence be likened to the hub of a wheel,
upon the outer rim of which some of the principal European cities are located.

Many travelers consider Brussels the third handsomest
capital in Europe, ranking it after Paris and Vienna. Certain
it is, that with its miles of superb boulevards, shaded by noble
trees and flanked by magnificent modern residences; its splen-
didly constructed pavements, washed and swept every night
with characteristic Flemish cleanliness; its Palace of Justice,
Conservatory of Music, Museum of the Fine Arts, and palatial
Bourse, in addition to its venerable Cathedral of St. Gudule,
the Hôtel de Ville, and other noble edifices of the past, it has
few rivals among the leading cities of the world.

The most interesting square in the Belgian capital is the
Place de l'Hôtel de Ville. Its history is almost identical with
that of Brussels; for hardly one remarkable event in the annals

of the city has lacked this area for its scene of action. What memories, therefore, cluster round the venerable buildings which front upon it.

On one side stands that beautiful specimen of Gothic architecture, known as the Hôtel de Ville, which still appears almost as stately and imposing as when its richly decorated walls sent back in noisy echoes the revelry of brilliant tournaments, or cast its shadow like a pall upon some cruel execution in the square below. This noble edifice suffered severely during the bombardment of the city by Louis XIV., in 1695, but the injured portions have been carefully restored after the original designs, and the result is one of the finest mediæval structures on the Continent. The most interesting apartment in this historic City Hall is the large banquet-room, which is adorned with fine oak carvings, and has a ceiling remarkable for the splendor of its ornamentation. It was here, in the fifteenth and sixteenth centuries, that the rich Flemish burghers

THE HÔTEL DE VILLE.

and the powerful Guilds of Brussels used to entertain, with pro-
verbial hospitality, the kings, dukes, princes, and ambassadors
who came to them from other lands. Nor is Belgian hospitality
a thing of the past. In 1890 when Henry M. Stanley was a
guest of the King of Belgium, immediately after the explorer's
return from his last trip through Africa, the Mayor and Alder-
men of Brussels gave a grand dinner in his honor in this ancient
banquet-room. It was a most interesting scene; for there were
gathered here, to meet the famous traveler, the ministers of England, France, the United States, and other great Powers, together
with representatives of the highest Belgian nobility, and the
leading men in the professional and literary life of the kingdom. Meantime, looking down on these distinguished guests
were the stern, impressive faces of William the Silent, Maurice
of Orange, Grotius, Egmont, Hoorn, and other Dutch and Flemish heroes, whose
noble portraits in
Gobelin tapestry
adorn the sombre
walls.

On the other
sides of the Grand
Place, as it is
often called, are
still to be seen a
number of impos-
ing buildings, con-
structed three
or four centuries
ago, yet well-
preserved, with
elaborate façades

HOUSE OF CHARLES V.

and Gothic roofs; and these, together with the Hôtel de Ville,
are eloquent reminders of the days when the rich and powerful

Flemish Guilds governed all Flanders, and brought their country to as high a position in respect to manufactures, military
prowess, material prosperity, and the fine arts as was attained
by any European nation of that age.

One of the most curious and interesting of these buildings
is known as the House of the King. This name, however, did

THE HOUSE OF THE KING.

not indicate a residence of royalty, in the usual sense of the
term, but merely signified the official residence of the King of
the Guilds, who, as the Chief of the Municipality, lived here
and entertained with sumptuous hospitality the city's guests;
for the liberty-loving Flemings held only a nominal allegiance
to the House of Austria, and practically knew no other king
than the chosen sovereign of their industrial Unions. Even

now in the active life of Brussels the Grand Place still holds a prominent position. It is not only the centre of all business pertaining to the Municipality, but it is also the site of some of the most interesting temporary markets that are held in the city. Once a week, for example, from six to nine o'clock in the morning, there will be found within this area a great bird market, when hundreds of canaries, nightingales, mocking-birds, thrushes, and parrots may be seen flitting about in their cages, chirping, singing, whistling, and filling the air with almost deafening, yet melodious, sounds. On such occasions, the square is chiefly occupied by the shrewd, jovial Flemish and Walloon peasant women, who are often somewhat boister-

ous in their eager-ness to exchange the silvery notes of their feathered songsters for the musical clink of silver coins. Twice a week, also, at the same hours, there is held here a flower market, and the whole square be-comes fragrant with the perfume of exquisite roses, carnations, and

ENTRANCE TO THE BOURSE.

other floral products brought in enormous quantities from the country districts. A visit to either of these markets, on a bright spring morning, is a charming experience, and gives a picture of the industrious habits, and the happy and contented life of the people, that will never fade from memory.

On one side of the Grand Place, in front of the House of the King, stood — until recently, when it was removed to a highly ornamented city park — an impressive monument commemorating the illustrious heroes of the Netherlands, Counts Egmont and Hoorn, who, on the 5th of June, 1568, were executed here by order of the Duke of Alva. These men, though Roman Catholics by birth and faith, had steadfastly opposed the cruel persecution of their countrymen by Philip II., and were on this account condemned to death. The execution of Egmont was unusually revolting, even for that age of pitiless severity, since it revealed the most shameful treachery and the blackest ingratitude on the part of the Spanish king. Count Philip Egmont was one of the loftiest types of knightly chivalry and soldierly charac- ter that Europe ever pro- duced, and he won for his ungrate- ful sover- eign, in a desperate conflict with the mar- shaled hosts of France, the brilliant victory of St. Quentin, in honor of which Philip had built the Escorial in Spain. Hence Eg-

EGMONT AND HOORN.

A BRUSSELS PARK.

mont's military renown and distinguished bravery were the pride of the Flemish race. William of Orange, his devoted friend, had repeatedly warned him of the treachery of Philip, and implored him to escape. But Egmont trusted both the Spanish sovereign and his perfidious agent, Alva, forgetting the popular proverb in regard to the former, "His dagger follows close upon his smile." When told of his inevitable doom, Egmont, despite his well-known courage,

was for a moment overwhelmed with horror and surprise, and exclaimed, " Alas! when I should think of God alone, I am unable to forget my wife and children." Then, recovering his composure, he remained calm and self-controlled until his death. A moment of profound silence succeeded the executioner's fatal stroke. Tears filled the eyes of many of the Spanish

MONUMENT TO ADMIRAL TROMP.

soldiers; for they had admired Egmont as a gallant warrior. The French ambassador, as he gazed upon the scene from a neighboring window, whispered: "There falls the head before which France has trembled twice." As for the people, notwithstanding the presence of the troops, they could not be restrained; and, rushing to the fatal block, they dipped their handkerchiefs in Egmont's blood, to thenceforth keep them as memorials of the crime, and as incentives to a terrible revenge.

GODFREY DE BOUILLON.

The monument erected to the memory of Egmont and to that of his loyal friend, Count Hoorn, is a reminder of the fact (too frequently forgotten) that, in the valorous resistance made by the Dutch against the cruel and colossal power of Spain, the Belgians joined with equal ardor and self-sacrifice; and, although not as successful as their neighbors, furnished nevertheless some of the grandest leaders in that mighty struggle, and many of the noblest martyrs to the sacred cause. The Flemish provinces, being easily reached, were quickly overrun by the well-trained troops of Spain, and consequently the Flemish people never had the same opportunities as the Hollanders for achieving victory; but Counts Egmont and Hoorn, together with many other brave compatriots, fully shared with William of Orange and Louis of Nassau the dangers and privations of that terrible war, and their immortal names are held to-day in solemn reverence throughout the realm.

Among the prettiest features of Brussels is the Place Royale, where one looks out from his hotel upon a handsome square, adorned with the equestrian statue of Godfrey de Bouillon, the hero of the first crusade. Brussels, like Paris, is not merely a gay, modern city; it has a background of impressive history. This statue, for example, represents the old crusader in the attitude which he assumed when, on this very spot, in 1097, he raised the standard of the Cross, and urged his fellow-countrymen to follow him to Palestine to rescue from the Saracens the sepulchre of Christ.

What an age of enthusiasm was that when such appeals drew multitudes away from home and kindred, to march thousands of miles, through endless difficulties and with no pecuniary recompense, to fight with desperate courage for an idea! It was the age that built cathedrals and worshiped God in forests made of stone; the age of chivalry, born of a reverence for the Madonna, which made all womanhood appear divine; and, above all, an age of sentiment, like that which caused the hero Godfrey, when elected King of Jerusalem, to refuse to wear a crown of gold in the city where his Saviour had worn a crown of thorns. Those days are gone. Cathedrals and crusaders would now be anachronisms. The ladies for whose glances mailèd knights contended in the tournament, or on the tented field, have been succeeded by the " New Woman." The narrow, mediæval river of intolerance, curbed by

the granite walls of dogma (and hence impetuous in its pent-up fury) has reached the open sea whose waves touch distant shores, and whose horizon steadily recedes as we advance. We can no more go back to the old age of simple faith and ardent zeal, than

THE BOURSE.

THE FRONT OF THE PALACE OF JUSTICE.

can the stream return from the broad ocean to its mountain channel; and yet, we sigh for something we have lost, and with an
irrepressible yearning for a resurrection of enthusiastic faith and
feeling, we agree with Holmes that "it is faith in something, and
enthusiasm for something, that makes a life worth looking at."

One of the finest modern buildings in the Belgian capital is
the Bourse, which was completed in 1774 at a cost of a million
dollars. It seemed to me, at first, incredible that such an
elegant edifice, elaborately adorned with Corinthian columns,
allegorical statues, and beautiful reliefs, could be merely the
Stock Exchange; yet it is characteristic of the city. Brussels
is wealthy. Belgium is progressive. It cannot boast of an
extensive territory, but it is determined to make the little that
it does possess not only prosperous but beautiful. As an illustration of its enterprise, it is worthy of note that this most

densely populated country in Europe was the first on the Continent to establish a system of railways.

The tourist in Belgium may well ask himself, therefore, "In the present condition of Europe is not a small, well-governed monarchy like this much better off than larger ones which must maintain enormous standing armies, and are continually fearing war?" The policy of Belgium seems to be: "Let others shake the tree; I will pick up the fruit."

The splendor of the Brussels Bourse is now surpassed by that of the new Palace of Justice, the cost of which was more than ten million dollars. It would be difficult to find in any city a secular building more magnificent and imposing. It forms an enormous rectangle, each side of which measures about six hundred feet, while in the centre rises a well-proportioned tower, four hundred feet in height. The question naturally suggests itself: How there can be in such a tiny realm as Belgium enough judicial business to make so huge a structure necessary. It is a striking illustration of the fact that while the other European nations have been wasting life and treasure on the battle-field, or carrying enormous burdens in preparation for war, Belgium

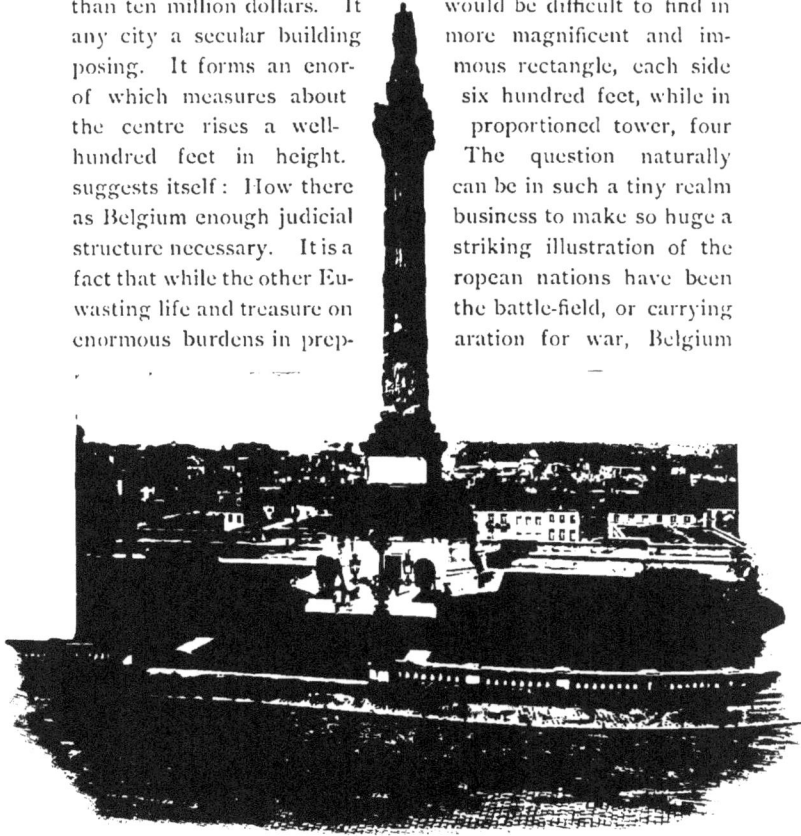

THE COLUMN OF CONGRESS.

THE BASE OF THE COLUMN.

has been employed in peaceful industries, and the most splendid and conspicuous building in her capital, today, is not an arsenal for her soldiers, nor even a fortress for defense, but a palatial temple for the goddess of justice.

Almost every European capital is embellished by at least one lofty shaft, characteristic of the nation and commemorative of its history. In London, it is Nelson's column in Trafalgar Square; in Paris, the Napoleonic column in the Place Vendôme; Berlin is dominated by her recent Monument of Victory; and in St. Petersburg we find the noble monolith which bears the name of Alexander I. The Belgian capital, also, has a historic column, worthy to be compared with those of other lands. It was erected to commemorate the founding of the kingdom in 1831, when its present liberal constitution was adopted, and Prince Leopold of Saxe-Coburg was elected king. A statue of this sovereign (the father of the reigning monarch) crowns the summit of the column at a height of two hundred and eighty-five feet; and at the corners of the pedestal are four bronze figures, which symbolize the basic principles of the government: Liberty of the Press, Liberty of Education, Liberty of Public Assemblage, and Freedom of Religious Worship. These are four elements from which we might expect an

almost perfect state to be constructed; and where in Europe
(all things considered) can we find a nation better governed,
a constitution more implicitly obeyed, a king more liberal and
progressive, and a people happier and more prosperous?

Leopold II. of Belgium is distinguished among other sovereigns of Europe for his unassuming manners and industrious
habits, as well as for the remarkable ability with which he con-
ducts the onerous and responsible duties of his high position.
I have been told by those who are well informed that he is the
busiest man in his kingdom.   He usually rises before six in
the morning, and may be seen soon after superintending the
rebuilding of his beautiful Château of Laeken, recently destroyed by fire, or consulting with his chief gardener over
the rare plants and flowers cultivated in his superb conservatory.   At nine o'clock he is in the palace at Brussels, and during the entire day is deeply engrossed in the affairs of State:
examining voluminous reports, consulting with his cabinet officers, receiving visits from ambassadors and other distinguished
people, making
plans for the
amelioration of
the inhabitants
of his Congo-
State, and for
the develop-
ment of its
commercial
life ; or em-
ployed in the
many details
which demand
the close atten-
tion of an en-
lightened and

MODERN BUILDINGS.

progressive ruler, desirous of securing the prosperity of his country and the welfare of his people. A brilliant diplomat, a shrewd, far-seeing statesman, liberal in all his ideas of government and administration, thoroughly in sympathy with the progressive ideas of the century, and sharing the hopes and aspirations of his people, King Leopold II. stands out conspicuous as one of the most eminent sovereigns of his time.

The Château of Laeken, the King's summer home, situated about three miles from Brussels, was, a few years ago, destroyed by fire. It was a most beautiful residence, and during the time when Belgium constituted a part of the Empire of France, under the first Napoleon, it was a favorite abode of the Emperor whenever he visited that part of his dominions. A friend of mine was recently honored with an invitation to dine with the King at Laeken, and, after the repast, as the King and Queen were strolling with their guests through some of the most interesting rooms of the château, Leopold II. suddenly stopped, and remarked, "This is historically a very interesting apartment, for from this room and from that little table in the centre began the downfall of Napoleon." To my friend, who inquired how this could be, the King replied: "In this room and on that table the Emperor Napoleon wrote his declaration of war against Russia, in 1812, from which moment I consider, dates the commencement of his downfall." When this château was burned, the King and royal family were at the palace in Brussels, holding their New Year's reception. The grenadiers on guard at Laeken, seeing that the

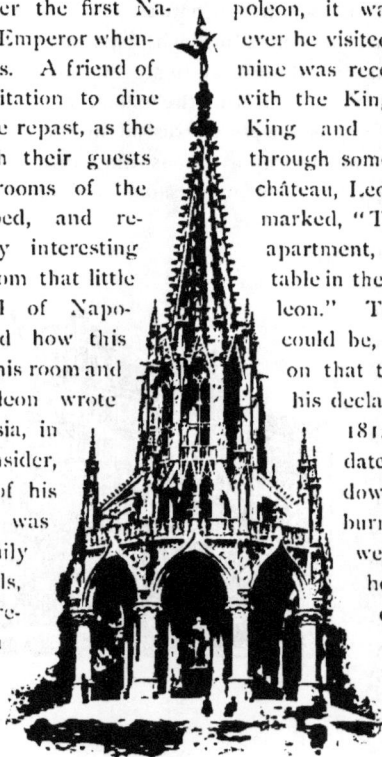

building was doomed, and knowing how
highly Leopold II. prized the Napoleon
table, made extraordinary efforts to
force their way into the building
through fire, smoke, and falling
timbers to secure it, and, finally,
to the great delight of the King,
succeeded in rescuing it before
it had been injured.

The Queen of Belgium is a
Princess of the House of Hapsburg,
and like most of the ladies of her
family is a famous horsewoman.   In
fact, for many years she was in the habit
of herself breaking in the wild Hungarian

THE QUEEN OF BELGIUM.

horses brought to Brussels for her use.   When "Buffalo Bill"
with his troop of Cowboys and Indians was in Belgium, in 1891,
he gave entertainments in Brussels for two weeks, and the
Queen, accompanied by a large number of the nobility, attended
several of his exhibitions.   Before leaving Brussels, Colonel Cody
with a few friends obtained the privilege of visiting the superb
Winter Garden of the King at Laeken.   After spending two
hours very pleasantly in this conservatory, which is one of
the finest in Europe, as they were about to leave, they saw
the Queen approaching, accompanied by officers and ladies of
her suite.   She graciously asked the gallant scout if he would
not like to see her stables and horses, and on receiving an
affirmative reply, this democratic sovereign personally conducted the party through her royal stables, going into the
stalls herself, leading out her favorite thoroughbreds, com-
menting on their fine points, and in every way showing her
intimate knowledge of horses and horsemanship.

This reference to "Buffalo Bill" and his associations with
royalty recalls an amusing circumstance connected with the

visit made to Berlin by this distinguished representative of
American frontier life. It happened that at the time of Colonel Cody's advent into the capital of Germany, old Emperor
William was entertaining there three kings of the smaller
Germanic powers. One feature of "Buffalo Bill's" perform-
ance is the exhibition of the antiquated Deadwood coach, containing passengers who are attacked by Indians and rescued
by Cowboys. The Kaiser asked to be allowed to ride in
this vehicle with his royal guests, and
to par- ticipate in this interesting experience.
The request was
of course granted,
and when the
coach was
fiercely as-
sailed by howl-
ing Indians,
its inmates
were as usual
saved by the
gallant Cowboys.
After it was over, and
as the royal party was
descending from the coach,
the Emperor remarked,

THE CHAMBER OF DEPUTIES.

"Colonel Cody, I don't suppose this is the first time that you
have held four kings?" "No, your Majesty," replied the quick-
witted scout, "you are right, but it is the first occasion that I
ever held four kings and the royal joker at the same time."

The level plains of Belgium have furnished Europe with its
battle-fields for many centuries. From the time of the Franks
under Clovis, down to the siege of Antwerp, in 1830, the wars
of western Europe have, to a large extent, been fought out in

PALACE OF JUSTICE, BRUSSELS.

Flanders. Within a radius of fifty miles of Brussels there are
at least twenty-five broad plains, which offer admirable ground
for the maneuvering of large armies. Hence, notwithstanding
the fact that the neutrality of Belgium is guaranteed by the five
great Powers, the Belgian government is so fearful lest this
little country should be invaded either from the East or West,
in case of war between France and Germany, that, of late years,
it has constructed along the Meuse and Sambre a continuous

line of powerful
steel forts, in
order to defend
the country and
to protect its neu-
trality. These
forts somewhat
resemble our tur-
ret monitors, be-
ing manipulated
by powerful ma-
chinery which
causes them to
disappear below
the surface of the
ground after dis-
charging their

NAMUR ON THE SAMBRE.

tremendous guns. They are well located at strategic points
along the two rivers, and, in case of war, would prove a serious
obstacle to an invading army. They were designed by the distinguished Belgian military engineer, General Brialmont, who,
a few years ago, was sent for by the Sultan to plan extensive
fortifications along the Dardanelles, and whose works on
modern defenses are used as text-books in our artillery school
at Fortress Monroe.

The question, whether it would be possible to preserve the

neutrality of Belgium in case of war between France and some
other Continental Power, is extremely interesting. It is well
understood that this neutrality has been guaranteed by England, France, Russia, Prussia, and Austria; yet, from a military
standpoint, it is also clear that the powerful armies likely to be
organized upon its borders, in case of war, would be compelled
to enter Belgium in order to secure a position in which to
attack each other. The fact is not generally known that at the
outbreak of hostilities between France and Germany, in 1870,
each of these Powers was promptly informed by the English
government that, when the first soldier of either
army entered the terri- tory of Belgium with
hostile intent, Great
Britain would imme-
diately intervene
with her entire land
and sea forces. Still,
notwithstanding the
well-known views of
England on this sub-

THE COACH TO WATERLOO.

ject, and the policy she would be likely to pursue to maintain
Belgian neutrality, I recently heard a distinguished European
diplomat say that if war should break out between France and
Germany, the neutrality of neither Belgium nor Switzerland
would be respected by either of the contending forces; that the
violation of neutral rights would be absolutely required by the
necessities of the situation; and that the contending armies
would undoubtedly be obliged to pass through one or both of
these neutral countries, or possibly even to fight on their soil.

The battle-ground in Belgium which is of most importance
in the history of Europe is that of Waterloo. It is situated
about thirty miles from Brussels, and can be easily reached
by rail, or by a coach which leaves the city every morning
for the battle-field, returning in the afternoon. The best

advice that I can
give a tourist who
wishes to see
Waterloo with
either pleasure or
profit, is to hire
one of the local
guides, in order
to escape their
importunity, and
then to pay him
something extra
to keep silent.
A few questions
about the topog-

BIRD'S-EYE VIEW OF WATERLOO.

raphy of the country and the positions of the armies will
naturally be asked, and will receive intelligent replies; but the
abominable "story of the battle" which ignorant guides nar-
rate, with changes suited to the nationality of the visitor, is
exasperating. Hard, indeed is the fate of the tourist who

is conducted
over the
scene of con-
flict with a
company of
strangers,
whose inap-
propriate re-
marks and
vehement ar-
guments are
particularly
annoying at
such a time.

LA BELLE ALLIANCE.

HEROES' MOUND, WATERLOO.

Waterloo is a place for reverie and solitude; and to behold it with a crowd of uncongenial travelers, or even with a loquacious guide who glibly states, as facts, things which have been disputed by the greatest military students of the world, is a misfortune. My first visit to Waterloo was spoiled by just such circumstances, and I have never ceased to regret it.

The battle-field of Marathon, in Greece, on the contrary, in its sublime and solemn isolation between the mountains and the sea, is almost an ideal spot for a poet, scholar, or historian, and the memory of a day passed there beside its "Heroes' Mound" is one of the most satisfactory experiences of my life.

There is also a Heroes' Mound at Waterloo. Two hundred feet in height, and surmounted by a colossal lion, it dominates the landscape from afar, and marks the centre of the battle-field. Most travelers do nothing more at Waterloo than climb the mound and take a general view of the his-

toric plain; but the ideal way to see the place where was,
at last, decisively concluded the duel between Napoleon and
United Europe, is to drive in a private carriage to its principal points of interest, and leisurely, and with appreciative
study, to inspect such objects as the farmhouse of La Belle
Alliance, where the Emperor had his headquarters; the site
of the sunken road which proved the grave of hundreds of
Napoleon's cavalry; the farm of La Haye Sainte, taken and
retaken three times on that eventful day; and, above all, the
old Château of Hougomont, against the thick stone walls of
which the reckless fury of the French attack hurled itself
desperately all day long, only to break in vain on the un-
yielding ramparts, like billows upon a rocky coast.

It is not necessary to recount the thrilling story of the battle.
It has been told in every language of the civilized world, and
many volumes have been written in explanation of its strategy
and its result. Suffice it here to say, the plans of the two com-
manders were simple. That of Wellington was to hold his

HOUGOMONT.

ground until the Prussians under Blücher should join him; that
of Napoleon was to defeat the English before the Prussians
could arrive, and then to annihilate Blücher. To this end, he
had dispatched Marshal Grouchy, with thirty thousand men, to
keep the Prussian army in check till he had finished with the
English. By a strange fatality, therefore, the issue of the conflict was destined to rest ultimately not with Napoleon and
Wellington, but with Grouchy and Blücher. In this tremendous crisis, the Frenchman failed; the Prussian succeeded.

THE CLOSE OF THE BATTLE.

Just as it was
evident that the
troops of Wel-
lington, if un-
aided, were
doomed to defeat,
the force of Blü-
cher arrived upon
the field. It was
half-past seven
o'clock, and twi-
light was ap-
proaching. The
French were now
outnumbered by
fifty thousand
men. The des-
tinies of Europe hung in the balance. Napoleon's fate depended on the charge of the Old Guard. Approaching these
companions in so many glorious victories, the Emperor uttered,
for the last time, the words, "*La Garde, En avant!*" The
veterans were commanded by Marshal Ney, the "Bravest of the
Brave," who, having already had five horses shot under him,
now advanced on foot. The heroes turned a farewell glance
toward their loved Emperor. Like the old gladiators of the

Colosseum, they might have cried, "O, Cæsar, we, who are about to die, salute thee!" For soon, beneath a deadly cross-fire of shot and shell, they seemed to melt like frost-work in the sun. The rest of the army gave way; a mortal pallor overspread Napoleon's face, and he attempted to ride on to death. But he was pushed back by his officers; and one of them, grasping the bridle of his horse, led him at full gallop from the first overwhelming defeat that he had ever known.

NEY.

"Be sure and stop at Ghent," a friend had said to us as we were leaving Brussels, "if you would see a genuine Flemish city of the olden time." When we beheld its picturesque old gateway, we rejoiced that we had taken his advice; for its pointed towers, pierced with narrow loopholes, and its gabled roof, rising like flights of steps to the high station of the sentinels, still fling their shadows across the ancient moat, just as they did when Ghent was the proud capital of Flanders, and from out this gate the warlike Ghentians marched to rout the English army under Edward I.

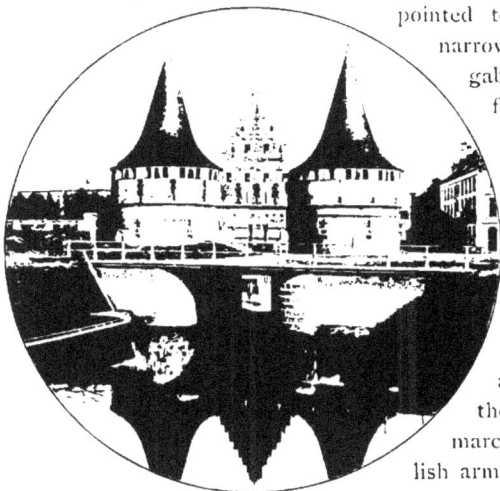

THE GATE, GHENT.

STATUE OF ARTEVELDE.

Especially interesting, from its historic associations, is the old market-place of Ghent, the forum of the Flemish capital. Here, homage was paid to the Counts of Flanders in a magnificence of style, rare at the present day even to royalty; and here, during the civil feuds, which were as desperate in Ghent as in mediæval Florence, the different factions would assemble, fierce to avenge some real or fancied violation of their rights. In one such contest alone fifteen hundred men were slain.

The statue in the centre of this square is that of Jacques Van Artevelde, the celebrated Brewer of Ghent, who, though of noble family, enrolled himself in the Guild of Brewers, that he might

ST. NICHOLAS CHURCH.

thus obtain the favor of the lower classes. Rich, eloquent, and able, he quickly rose to be for eight years the virtual sovereign of Flanders, putting to death or banishing those who ventured to oppose him, and filling all the offices with men obedient to his will; yet, near this square, where, with uplifted arm he had so often roused the populace to further his designs, he was at last assassinated by the very men who, while admiring his genius, would not brook his despotism.

Leaving this historic site, a short walk brought us to the oldest church in Ghent, founded nine hundred years ago. Around its base, like barnacles upon a stately ship, have gathered several small shops, which should be cleared away; but, in spite of these, the building has a rugged

ST. BAVON ABBEY.

grandeur suited to its history. Its pointed turrets were already old when, in the time of the Crusaders, a Flemish Count brought back to decorate the summit of the neighboring spire a gilded dragon taken from the church of Santa Sophia at Constantinople; and they looked grimly down upon the lurid fires which in this square consumed so many victims of the Duke of Alva, the cruel minister of Philip II.

Leaving this church, we walked a little distance to some mediæval cloisters of rare beauty. Through their deserted walls the winds of centuries have blown, but they retain suffi-

cient traces of their noble architecture to show us what they
must have been. Alas! like many other historic structures in
the Netherlands, these cloisters were defaced and sacked by
Puritan fanatics; for in those dreadful days — when the
Inquisition was making this fair land a place of fiendish torture and unutterable misery, goaded by years of persecution and
looking upon all such architecture as emblematic of the power
which persecuted them — a multitude of image breakers, armed
with ropes and hammers, swept like a whirlwind through the
realm. The dam-
age done by these
iconoclasts was
irreparable. In
the cathedrals,
statues were
hurled from their
pedestals, and
paintings were
torn from the
walls; glorious
stained-glass win-
dows were shiv-
ered to atoms;
ladders and ropes
were used to

CLOISTER OF ST. BAVON.

reach the works of art, and lofty pinnacles and turrets,
apparently inaccessible, were scaled by men who risked their
lives to mar their beautiful decorations. Revolting scenes of
sacrilege took place. Statues of Christ were thrown down
with the rest; those of the Virgin suffered every insult; the
sacred altars were defiled; the consecrated wine was drunk;
the sacramental bread was thrown to dogs, and even the oil
with which kings and priests had been anointed was used by
these fanatics to grease their shoes. In one night thirty

HISTORIC HOUSES, BRUGES.

churches were sacked in Antwerp alone, and four hundred
were despoiled in a single province within a few days. Thus,
through a religious frenzy, easily understood, yet evermore to
be regretted, the precious products of centuries of inspiration
and persistent labor were completely ruined, and once more, as
so many times before, the world was rendered poorer by the
folly and bigotry of man.

A striking incident is told of a wealthy, though untitled,
citizen of Ghent. One day, the mighty Emperor Charles V.,
needing two mil-
lion florins, bor-
rowed them all of
this worthy man;
and the same day,
in token of his
gratitude, prom-
ised that he would
dine with him.
The flattered mer-
chant gave the
Emperor a most
magnificent re-
past; and, while
they sipped their
wine at the des-

THE PULPIT.

sert, tore up the monarch's promissory note and passed the
pieces to him on a plate. "Sire," he said, "two million florins
is a small sum to pay for the honor which your Majesty has
done me to-day."

Musing upon the history of this Flemish city, once so
famous for its wealth and power, I fancied I could see moving
along its liquid thoroughfares, like phantoms of the past, the
stately ships from India and Persia, bringing to Ghent the
treasures of the Orient. Once more I watched march proudly

through the city's
streets its famous
manufacturing
guilds, a single
one of which
numbered forty
thousand men. I
saw its artisans
pass by in such
vast crowds that,
when the bells
were rung at
morning, noon,
and night, all
other citizens

OLD FLEMISH HOUSES.

were warned not to obstruct the living current sweeping on its
way. Vessels, meantime, were not allowed to pass the drawbridges, which were kept closed for the accommodation of the
moving throng, and children were retained indoors, lest the

A GATE, BRUGES.

industrial hosts should
trample them to death.
Larger than Paris even
was this city in those days,
and Charles V. had some
justification for his famous
pun on the French name
of Ghent, when he said to
the King of France, " I can
put your Paris inside of
my glove " (*Je mettrai votre
Paris dans mon Gand*).

Saying farewell to
Ghent, an hour's journey
brought us to her former

rival, — Bruges. There is no rivalry between the cities now.
Ghent, though retaining but a shadow of her ancient glory,
is still comparatively prosperous; but poor old Bruges shows
little evidence of life and enterprise. Some stately buildings
of the past remain, which give to her an air of wealth and
dignity, and the old streets and market-places are, in form,
the same; but few boats furrow now her deep canals, which,
with the green scum floating on their stagnant surfaces, resemble unused country roads, half overgrown with grass. Even

the numerous
bridges of the
town, which gave
to her the Flem-
ish title, Bruges,
look lifeless and
deserted, and
most of the oc-
cupants of the
handsome houses
of the olden time
are wealthy mer-
chants who have
retired from busi-
ness, to spend the
last years of their

AN OLD CANAL, BRUGES.

lives in absolute tranquillity. There seems to be no danger
of its being disturbed.

I could not see that any business, save a little petty traffic,
was transacted here, and it is said that nearly one-third of the
inhabitants of Bruges are paupers. Beggars and guides
annoyed us so persistently that, in self-defence as well as pity,
we finally hired a "*commissionaire*," and gave all our spare
pennies to the mendicants. I think we also saved a wretched
cabman from committing suicide, by hiring his dilapidated vehi-

cle at the astonishing price of twenty-five cents an hour! Cabs are, in fact, so cheap and slow in Bruges that I should have taken one from morning till night, if I had only had plenty of time.

Shaken about in one of these decrepit vehicles, driven over atrocious cobble-stone pavements, yet cheered by our approving consciences for having thus encouraged industry, we entered the old marketplace and looked upon the famous belfry of Bruges. It is a majestic structure, three hundred and fifty feet in height, richly adorned with fine stone-carving, and ending in a lofty octagon, whose open-work balcony commands a noble view. A portion of the edifice from which it rises is still a government office, but part of it has now degenerated into a meat market. Times change, indeed, and we change with them. This tower, built more than five hundred years ago, has played a prominent part in the eventful history of Bru-

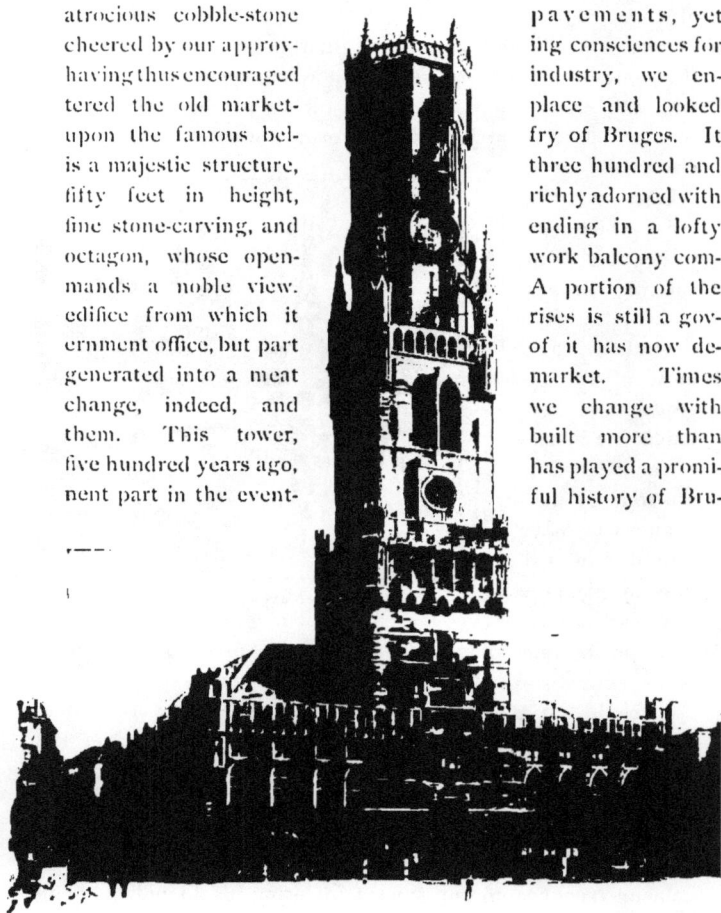

OLD CANAL AND STREET.

ges, and when its time-honored chimes ring out upon the air, one can imagine them trying to arouse the lifeless city to a realization of her former glory; reminding her that in the fifteenth century she was wealthier than even Antwerp; that ships from Venice, Genoa, and the distant East unloaded here their precious cargoes; that once, as a result of civil war, two hundred wagons were kept busy for a fortnight transporting loads of gold, silver, and valuable goods to the victorious city, Ghent; that twenty foreign ministers lived then within her gates; that here a German King was held prisoner twelve days, despite the threats of royal armies; and that the Queen of France, on seeing the splendid dresses of the ladies of Bruges, exclaimed, "I thought that I alone was Queen, but here are hundreds whose costumes rival mine." Moreover, it was the people of Bruges who

THE CITY HALL, BRUGES.

ANTWERP HARBOR.

dared to say to the ambassador of France, "Go tell your King that he is perjured, that we have elected a new sovereign, and that it is our privilege, not his, to choose our masters."

It is difficult to realize the prosperity which the Netherlands enjoyed three hundred years ago; but they supplied Charles V. with nearly one-half of his royal income: four times as much as was furnished by Spain, or by those Eldorados of the New World, — Mexico and Peru. The Low Countries then contained more than two hundred walled cities, all of which were in a flourishing condition. In all these towns belfries were constructed, fully as much for secular as for sacred purposes. In times of peace, it is true, they musically chimed the passing hours, and called the worshiper to prayer; but they were also deep-voiced sentinels, whose brazen clangor summoned citizens to arms, and brought them at a moment's notice, rushing from the remotest lanes, into the central square.

The name, Antwerp, is said to be derived from Flemish words which signify, "On the Wharf." If so, the title is appropriate, for it is on the wharves of Antwerp that the prosperity of the city is best understood. It is a town of great activity, and its superb quays — built by Napoleon I., when Antwerp formed a prominent part of his colossal empire — are

crowded now with ships and steamers, and serve as a reminder
of Bonaparte's gigantic plans and indefatigable industry.   Yet,
busy as Antwerp is to-day, it gives us but a hint of what its commerce was in the sixteenth century.   Then twenty-five hundred
ships could find shelter in its harbor, and it was no uncommon
occurrence for five hundred arrivals and departures to be regis-
tered in a single day.   Two thousand loaded wagons, also, from
the neighboring provinces passed daily through the city's
gates; and in addition to Antwerp's own commercial houses,
more than a thousand foreign firms contended here in friendly
rivalry.   No city in all Christendom could equal Antwerp then
in wealth and splendor.   Her merchants lived in almost regal
luxury; within her massive warehouses were precious goods
from every land; and her superb cathedral, palaces, and public
buildings, enriched with noble works of art, made her the
marvel of the world.

But, alas! when did so great a treasure ever long escape the
clutch of the despoiler?   The Spaniards coveted this goodly
city, and laid
upon it the same
cruel hand that
proved a curse to
all their colonies
in   the   New
World.   In the
capture of Ant-
werp by the
Spanish army
almost as many
living beings
were destroyed as
there had been
statues ruined in
the memorable

THE HOUSE OF RUBENS.

THE INTERIOR OF THE BOURSE.

image breaking of ten years before. The annals of the Netherlands are illustrated by some of the most horrible pictures
known to history; and one of the most revolting is that of
the sack of Antwerp by the Spaniards. In three days, fully
eight thousand men, women, and children were massacred,
burned, or drowned, and bodies lay by hundreds in the streets.
The Spanish soldiers, drunk with wine and blood, had cast off
even the semblance of humanity, and played the part of fiends.
The splendid city was well-nigh destroyed. Six million dollars'
worth of property was burned, and five hundred marble residences were reduced to blackened ruins. The object of these
terrible atrocities was gold, and to obtain it almost inconceivable
cruelties were committed. To cite one out of many instances:
a wedding feast was being celebrated when the Spaniards
gained possession of the city. A mob of brutal soldiers rushed
within the house, demanding gold and jewels. Not satisfied
with what they found, they struck the bridegroom dead. The

bride fell, shrieking, into her mother's arms, whence she was torn by the relentless ruffians, who immediately put the mother to death. The bride, who was of remarkable beauty, was then carried off. Maddened by this last outrage, her father tried to save her, and was killed. That night a woman, scantily clothed and trembling with fear, was found wandering through the streets among the heaps of dead and dying, looking for her husband and father. She was completely crazed; and the fair bride of a few hours before was finally put out of her misery by a mob of soldiers!

THE NATIONAL BANK AND LEOPOLD MONUMENT, ANTWERP.

VAN DYCK.

Before the bar of History no nation has committed such atrocious crimes, or brought such evil upon millions of the world's inhabitants as Spain. Her terrible expulsion of the gifted Moors and wealthy Jews was one of the most deadly blows ever given to learning, art, and commerce, aside from its appalling cruelty and bigotry; the record of her conquests and tyrannical government in the New World has left on every foot of soil that she occupied a sickening trail of blood; and, while she ruled the Netherlands, she made the lives of its inhabitants a hell on earth, by pillaging cities, slaughtering, torturing, and burning thousands of innocent men, women, and children, and lighting every market-place with the fires of the Inquisition. In the whole history of mankind there is no sadder and more awful picture than that of the decline and wretchedness of this superbly prosperous and artistic country under the rule of Spain. Thousands abandoned the Netherlands and fled to England, and thousands who remained were put to death by fire and sword. In 1568 Antwerp had a population of one hundred and twenty-five thousand. Twenty years later its inhabitants numbered only fifty-five thousand. Since then, till recently, a series of misfortunes, including wars, political vicissitudes, revolutions, and unfortunate maritime decrees, has kept it from recovering its former prosperity. At present, however, it is rapidly regaining its lost fortunes, and if it has half a century more of peace, under as good a government as that of Leopold II., it will take long strides toward regaining the position it once occupied, — that of the leading maritime city.

Antwerp's cathedral spire has held the admiration of the world for centuries, and well deserves the eulogy of Napoleon.

THE CATHEDRAL, ANTWERP.

who compared it to a piece of Mechlin lace. On account of the
flatness of the surrounding country, it is visible at a great distance, long before the rest of the town is seen, and the impression which it makes on the approaching tourist, who, as he sails
along the winding Schelde, watches this solitary shaft of stone
embroidery cutting its slender silhouette upon the sky, will not
be easily forgotten. Its airy pinnacles contain about one hundred bells — the smallest sixteen inches in circumference, the
largest weighing eight tons — and from these there floats out
upon the air a combination of melodious sounds scarcely surpassed, I think, in Europe. It is hard to realize that this graceful tower was standing, in peaceful beauty, through all the
dreadful scenes of carnage which have stained the history of
Antwerp, and that its chimes rang out as sweetly then as now,
above the shouts of triumph and the moans of anguish in the
streets below. Aside from its bell-tower, however, the cathe-

THE STATUE OF RUBENS.

dral of Antwerp
is disappointing.
Not only has the
space surround-
ing it been in-
vaded by a num-
ber of mean
buildings, but the
effect of the in-
terior is sadly
marred by the
presence of
whitewashed
walls and col-
umns. Still, as
the spire redeems
the exterior, so
the interior of

THE "ELEVATION OF THE CROSS" (RUBENS)

the church is atoned for, and even endeared to lovers of art,
by the two masterpieces of Rubens which hang on either side
of the high altar : the " Elevation of the Cross," and the " Descent from the Cross."

We climbed to the lofty belfry of the cathedral, and
looked down on the city and the adjoining plain; and, as we

watched the river Schelde winding through cultivated fields,
like a long thread of silver woven in a figured carpet, we
were reminded of a striking proof of bravery connected with
this peaceful stream.   In 1831, during the war between the
Dutch and Belgians, a Holland gunboat was driven ashore
here in a heavy gale.   The Belgian men-of-war at once surrounded it, and summoned its commander to surrender.   Seeing that further opposition was impossible, and yet determined
never to give up what had been entrusted to his care, the
captain rushed to the powder magazine, threw into it a lighted
match, and, in a moment more, a terrible explosion wrecked
the ship and killed a hundred of the advancing enemy.
Thus did this officer, who in childhood had been adopted by
the state, and had received his education at government
expense, nobly repay the debt he owed his country; and, in
her turn, Holland showed her gratitude by rearing a monument to his memory, and ordering that one vessel in
her navy should   always   bear
his   honored   name.

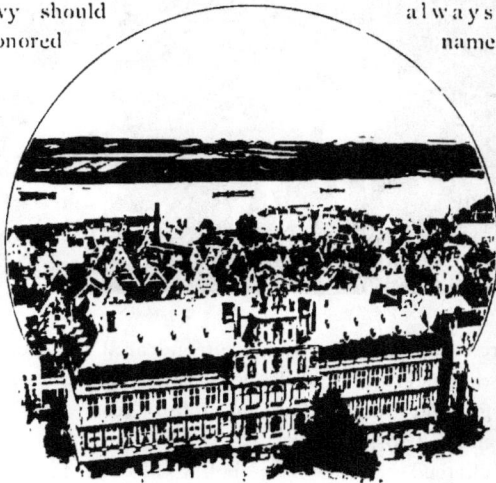

ANTWERP AND THE SCHELDE.

HOLLAND

HOLLAND

I SHALL never forget my first experience in Holland. How eagerly and laughingly we gazed about us at our new surroundings. Was it, then, possible that land could be as flat as this? At times, I fancied it a smooth green carpet, dotted here and there with windmills which looked like pegs designed to keep tapestry in place; at other times, the country seemed like a gigantic raft, which nothing but the constant efforts of its mariners could keep afloat. In view of this uninterrupted area of level territory, who would be much surprised if the Dutch government should stamp upon its coins the motto recently chosen by a youthful bride to ornament her suite of rooms, "God bless our flat"? Rising from such

RAILWAY AND CANAL.

HOLLAND COWS.

a level founda-
tion, buildings in
Holland appear
tall and windmills
monstrous. Even
the cows look
larger than those
of other lands,
and, quite in har-
mony with their
surroundings,
have flat horns.
They are sleek,
handsome crea-
tures, such as the
Flemish painters have portrayed so often, and stand in groups
upon the velvet turf, whose verdant surface has a glow as soft
as that of porcelain. These herds of happy cattle were as
sedate as their
owners, and made
no effort to run
away when we
approached, but
merely gazed in
large-eyed won-
der at our passing
train.

Holland is
not usually con-
sidered a beauti-
ful country, but
it possesses one
peculiar charm of
scenery that I

A LOVELY LANDSCAPE.

have never seen surpassed. The flatness and extent of its
broad, green meadows by the sea permit unusually long per-
spectives, under the lowering clouds, to the very verge of the
horizon, much as the traveler finds them on the ocean. At
such a time, the sight of cattle, trees, and windmills etched
boldly on the band of light which intervenes between the
clouds and the horizon line is wonderfully effective; and I
have rarely seen in any landscape more fascinating pictures
than Holland can reveal upon a showery afternoon, when, as
the clouds drift by, the windmills, cows, and meadows dissolve
into a silvery mist, and, a few minutes later, reappear through
a pale, shimmering veil of gray and gold. No land has ever
been more faithfully portrayed in art than Holland, and many
times a day the traveler in the Netherlands sees duplicates of
scenes which the old Dutch painters have immortalized.

The two most characteristic features
of Holland are its windmills and canals.

TIRELESS LABORERS.

The former seem innumerable. In fact, the country often appears to be alive with these revolving monsters, which, when in motion, look like giants turning handsprings on the horizon; and, when at rest, resemble lighthouses above the sea. But "rest" for these industrious slaves is a rare occurrence. Employed for almost every kind of labor, they grind corn, saw wood, pulverize rock, manufacture paper, and cut tobacco into snuff; while their most important duty is to pump out of the marshes into the canals the water which would otherwise submerge the land. Think of an army of ten thousand of these tireless *automata* working continually, day and night, to raise the liquid of the lowlands high enough to let it find an exit to the sea! The largest windmills, it is said,

A DUTCH WATERWAY.

will, in a fair breeze, lift ten thousand gallons of water per minute to the height of four feet.

Who can refuse unstinted admiration to the persevering Hollanders, who have thus yoked the inconstant wind and forced it not only to work for them, but also to contend with their great enemy, water? It is true, the windmills often look rebellious, and fling their long arms madly round and round, as if in frantic protest at their slavery; but, nevertheless, they faithfully perform their allotted tasks, and are a practical illustration of the rough but wholesome words of Emerson: "Bor-

HOLLAND WOMEN.

row the might of the
elements. Hitch your
wagon to a star, and
see the chores done
by the gods them-
selves." A Holland-
er's wealth is often es-
timated, not by bonds
and mortgages, but by
windmills. "How rich
is such a man?" I once
asked. "Ten or twelve
windmills," was the
answer.

A BIT OF HOLLAND.

The climax of Dutch ingenuity has been reached, however, in compelling the ocean — their natural enemy, which
threatens constantly to overwhelm them — to actually aid them
in repelling human foes; for, by an intricate system of locks
and sluices, they can inundate certain sections of the country,

A QUAINT STREET.

and either drown
or drive away in-
vaders. Small,
therefore, though
their army be, the
Hollanders have
a natural ally that
even the best-
trained European
soldiers cannot
conquer; and the
brave Dutch may
well exclaim to
any mightier na-
tion which shall

try to rob them of their independence, "One, with God, is a majority."

So profoundly uneventful seems Dutch existence, that I should think physicians would prescribe a residence in sleepy Holland as a cure for nervous prostration. In winter, however, life here must have some excitement. Without much snow, yet with a temperature often below the freezing-point, Holland is the paradise of skaters; and on the crystal paths which then bind all departments of the realm together as with silver cords, men, women, and children spend de-

HOLLAND IN WINTER.

lightful hours, having practically no limit to their wanderings; since they are able, if they choose, to glide for miles along these frozen highways, and visit in a short time, and with no cost of transportation, numerous towns and villages. Thus people often skate from Rotterdam to the Hague, and return the same day; in all, a distance of thirty miles. It is a common thing for boys and girls to skate to school, and even for Dutch ladies to make use of skates to do their marketing. Cities, too, institute ice carnivals, and invite their neighbors to join them in skating festivals.

The lower classes in Holland have an advantage in dress over their superiors, when skating; for their baggy trousers serve as sails, and when a plethoric Dutchman puts his hands in his pockets and expands his nether garments, so as to catch

the breeze, he rapidly leaves behind him those who are clad in
the conventional style. It should, however, be remembered
that these canals, when frozen, are not merely avenues of pleasure, but are also used as thoroughfares of transportation. Hence
skaters on them frequently encounter sledges, containing articles which would in summer be conveyed by boats.

Delighted with the oddity and beauty of Holland scenery,
we saw at last from our car window the city of Rotterdam.
This famous centre of Dutch commerce, fourteen miles from
the North Sea, lies at the union of two rivers, one of which
is called Rotter, and with the great dike, erected on its banks,
gives to the town the name of Rotter-dam. This is a clew by
which to comprehend all similar titles. Thus, Amster-dam
signifies the dam upon the Amstel; and the names Schiedam,
Zaändam, Edam, Durgedam, Volendam, and all the other
"dams" refer to dikes in their vicinity.

THE RAILROAD BRIDGE, ROTTERDAM.

DRAWBRIDGES, ROTTERDAM.

On my first walk in Rotterdam, I was bewildered by its multitude of bridges. From almost any halting-place I could count eight or ten; and, as most of them were drawbridges, they rose and fell like parts of an immense machine. Another feature of the town that seemed to me remarkable was the sign which I observed quite frequently above the doors of shops, " Fire and Water to sell." If it had read simply "Firewater," I might have concluded that Holland gin could there be bought; but "Fire *and* Water" puzzled me, until I learned that a regular trade is carried on here of selling to the poor hot peat and boiling water, with which to cook their frugal meals. Many boats are employed in bringing water to the city for sale.

A CANAL IN ROTTERDAM.

ROTTERDAM.

For, strange as it may seem, with a situation where land
and ocean struggle for supremacy, Rotterdam, as well as almost all the other Dutch cities, is in the condition of Cole-
ridge's Ancient Mariner, with "Water, water everywhere, nor
any drop to drink." I refer, however, to good drops. There
are, of course, stale, insipid, and malodorous drops; but pure,
sweet, wholesome water, the best gift of God, is not easily
found in the Low Countries. I was not much surprised, therefore, to see two men propelling through the various canals

a barge contain-
ing casks of drink-
ing water, which
they announced
by cries resem-
bling those of our
itinerant venders
of oranges and
strawberries.
People who have
no cisterns buy it
by the gallon; the
price, of course,
varying in times
of drought, or in
midwinter when

WATER BARGES.

the canals are frozen. It is not strange, then, that not far from
Rotterdam is a thriving town, in which three hundred distilleries
produce the finest gin the world affords. Personally speaking,
of all liquors, gin is the least attractive to my taste; but, as a
choice of evils, if I had for any length of time to imbibe the
natural water of Rotterdam, I certainly should be tempted to
disguise its taste with what the Dutch call *schnapps*.

Among other Dutch peculiarities, I noticed that almost
every man in Rotterdam had a cigar or pipe in his mouth.

The Hollanders are inveterate smokers. The boatmen, it is said, measure distances by smoke and reckon, not so many miles from place to place, but so many pipes. Some Dutchmen, it is alleged, go to sleep at night with their pipes between their lips, so that they may find them there the first thing in the morning, and light them before rising to the duties and trials of another day. Tobacco smoke is, therefore, called their second breath, and a cigar the sixth finger of their hands.

A DUTCH FLOWER MARKET.

This habit, combined with the peculiar climate, makes them the calmest, most phlegmatic people upon earth. Smoking in America's dry atmosphere excites and irritates; but among the Dutch canals it drugs and stupefies. In one of the streets of Rotterdam, I was shown the home of the greatest smoker that the world has known. Meinheer Van Klaes, as he was called, consumed, on the average, one hundred and fifty grams of tobacco every day, yet lived till he was ninety-eight years old. His last will and testament was extraordinary. After bequeathing most of his possessions to his relatives, he thus directed how he should be buried: "I wish that all my friends who are smokers shall be specially invited to my funeral. Each of them shall receive a package of tobacco and two pipes, and they are requested to smoke uninterruptedly during the funeral ceremonies. My body shall be enclosed in a coffin lined with the wood of my old cigar boxes. Beside me in the casket shall be laid my favorite meerschaum, a box of matches, and a package of tobacco. When my body is lowered into the grave, every person present is requested to pass by and cast upon it the ashes from his pipe." These touching requests, it is said, were faithfully complied with. His friends

A CHARACTERISTIC SCENE, ROTTERDAM.

attended in prodigious numbers; and, at the funeral, the smoke was so dense that a horn had to be blown to enable the mourners to find the door.

A COMMERCIAL CENTRE.

From this city of the champion smoker, we journeyed to the still more interesting Dutch metropolis, Amsterdam. This has been often called the "Venice of the North"; but the title is somewhat of a misnomer. It is true, there is a certain general resemblance between the cities, from the fact that Amsterdam is founded

upon ninety islands, furrowed by miles of liquid streets, spanned
by about three hundred bridges; moreover, the sea is in her
thoroughfares and laves the doorsteps of her shops and houses;
but there all likeness between Amsterdam and its Italian rival
ends. While the Dutch city calls forth admiration and respect,
the Adriatic Queen inspires a romantic sentiment akin to love.
Venice is golden; Amsterdam is gray. The City of the Doges

PANORAMA OF AMSTERDAM.

is poetical; that of the Dutch Burghers is prosaic. The southern city is voluptuous and tender, mysterious with her memories
of splendor and decay. The city of the North is cold and
practical, with a complacent air of solid worth and unimpeach-
able respectability.

The contrast between the cities is, perhaps, best shown by
the conveyances peculiar to each place. In Venice they are
those dusky spirits of the canals, — the slender, graceful gon-

THE ROYAL PALACE, AMSTERDAM.

dolas. In Amsterdam they are the heavy boats of traffic. The future of the cities, also, will be entirely different. Venice is dying like a gorgeous sunset; but Amsterdam, the rugged offspring of the northern sea, is, for its size, one of the wealthiest cities in the world; its bankers hold the securities of

A SIDE STREET IN AMSTERDAM

every nation, and on its broad canals float vessels from all quarters of the globe.

Many of the barges in Amsterdam form the abodes of

THE SHIPPING, AMSTERDAM.

people who have no other homes. Among a certain class of Hollanders, when a young man has saved or borrowed money enough he buys a huge, broad-shouldered boat; and, like the Patriarch Noah, leads into it not only his family, but also all the animals of which he is possessed, including poultry, hogs, and even cows. Thenceforth he is independent; and, as the master of a floating house, stable, farmyard, and express cart all in one, and never absent from his family, he transports loads of merchandise from town to town, and even sells a few superfluous eggs, or a little milk. What is most amusing is the way in which such an amphibious farmer, having moored his boat, takes his wares from house to house;

for he may be frequently observed standing without a blush of shame beside the only vehicle I ever saw, that could be properly called a dog-cart! How often on my walks in Holland I have met peasants tramping along in whitewashed wooden shoes, beside a muzzled dog which some-

A DUTCH FAMILY.

times staggered, and frequently lay down from sheer exhaustion! It makes no difference what their size or breed may be, all dogs are forced to labor here unmercifully. My pity for them may be owing to the fact that in America dogs are regarded merely as pets; but I confess that I always felt, on observing Holland dogs compelled to draw heavy loads, much as I do at seeing children kept from play and made to labor in factories. Moreover, the work of Dutch dogs does not end, when the mer-

STATUE OF REMBRANDT, AMSTERDAM.

chandise is sold; for, when the
chance is offered him, the
driver seats himself in
the cart, which fre-
quently is heavy
enough for a small
pony, and makes his
wretched steeds draw
him home. It really
exasperated me to
see this treatment of
the canine race in Hol-
land. But the dogs are
cheap, and the men are

CANINE USEFULNESS.

either lazy or hard-hearted; hence, so long as no society exists
there to prevent it, man's most devoted friend and trusty comrade will probably be compelled to lead a worse existence than
is indicated by our expression, "A dog's life!"

Sometimes, however, Hans does not own a dog. What
then? Does he assume the load himself? O, no! He puts
it on his wife. "Gretchen," he
says, "bring me my pipe,
like a good *hausfrau*, and
I will help you get the
yoke upon your shoul-
ders." Then, while he
calmly sits upon the
deck, a halo of to-
bacco smoke about
his head, his patient
spouse goes on her
way, like the mere
beast of burden
that she is. I

DOG DAYS.

GOING TO MARKET.

wonder if she ever asks the question, "Is marriage a failure?" Poor creature! We may laugh at her odd dress, her hat which looks like a wash basin inverted, and the huge bows of stiff, black cloth which stand out from her head like a bat's wings; but, after all, hers is a sad fate, and will continue to be till the Holland peasant rises to some sense of chivalry. It must be confessed, also, that Dutch husbands, in even the middle and upper classes of society, do not show excessive gallantry to their wives.

I shall not soon forget a conversation I once had with my landlady in Amsterdam. Amazed, apparently, at my expressions of sympathy for Holland dogs and peasant women, she said to me: "I am going to tell you something which I know will please you, and which is really true. Some years ago, an American gentleman and his wife were boarding with me. The lady was recovering from an illness, and one day her husband

HEAVILY LOADED.

A HOLLAND HEADDRESS.

wished her to take a drive. Now, what do you think he did? Why, when the horses were at the door, he took his wife up in his arms, carried her downstairs, and put her into the carriage. Nor was that all. When they returned, he took her in his arms again and carried her upstairs. There! Did you ever hear of such a thing as that? Was not the man a saint?"

"A saint!" I answered, "not at all, he was only an American."

The little houses in the vicinity of Amsterdam are thoroughly characteristic of Holland. Their sharply pointed roofs of bright red tiles, their neatly painted walls and blinds, a monstrous windmill on one side, and panting dogs on the other, — these are features of Dutch scenery which multiply themselves here almost endlessly. Stopping occasionally at one of these houses to inquire my way, I found the floors and tables scoured and polished, as if they had been sandpapered; the pots and pans glistened as if made of gold and silver; and in one room I noticed that all the chairs were tipped forward, with their hind feet on the top edge of the baseboard, so that the dust should not settle upon the seats in the short interval that could elapse between one dusting and another.

A COUNTRY SCENE.

Even in the better streets of Amsterdam, among the residences of its wealthy citizens, there is not much display of luxury. The houses are quite plain, though built of brick, and have stone trimmings at the doors and windows: a flight of steps leads sideways up to the front door, so as to take as little space as possible on the sidewalk; and the windows, of huge plate glass, are exquisitely polished. Outside of them are frequently mirrors, placed at such an angle as to reflect the scene below; for Hollanders lead such quiet lives that they are naturally curious to know all that goes on about them. The older houses with their pointed gables have, usually, above the attic window a beam and pulley hanging over the street. I jestingly called these at first a kind of gallows, on which the

Dutch of former times were wont to hang such thoughtless miscreants as dared intrude upon their polished floors with muddy feet. They were, in fact, invented as an aid to cleanliness; for by these pulleys are still hoisted into the attics all articles of household use

CHARACTERISTIC HOUSES, AMSTERDAM.

which might deface the immaculate front steps and halls.

I could not walk along these streets without inquiring what was done to prevent accidents by drowning. How can Dutch children, for example, ever play upon such narrow sidewalks without falling into the canals, and how can the men who have imbibed too freely of *schnapps* contrive to guide their reeling steps along these narrow spaces, which are unguarded by a parapet, and have the friendly lamp-posts few and far between? Yet I was told that deaths from drowning here are rare, partly

THE HOTEL AMSTEL, AMSTERDAM.

because the Dutch are naturally cautious; chiefly, no doubt, because long practice renders them as certain of their steps as Blondin on his swinging rope.

To a Dutchman it would seem impossible to have too much water about his house. Even with a canal in front and another on each side,

" NARROW SIDEWALKS."

he will add, if possible, an artificial pond in his small garden as a necessary adjunct to his comfort, and, if he builds a summer-house, he will, by preference, locate it over a canal.

From Amsterdam we journeyed to the beautiful Dutch capi-

A LIQUID AVENUE.

tal,—the Hague. It is a charming place; not quite so odd as Amsterdam and Rotterdam, since the majority of its streets are not canals; but it has all the best peculiarities of Holland, without an undue prominence of water and unsavory

THE PALACE OF JUSTICE, THE HAGUE.

odors. Indeed, I think there is not in the whole of Europe, from Lisbon to St. Petersburg, a cleaner and more aristocratic city than the Hague. Its site was formerly a densely wooded hunting park belonging to the Counts of Holland, which gave the town that subsequently rose here its quaint Dutch title: "'s Graven Hage," or the Count's Garden.

As a rule, the architecture of the Hague is not only solid and substantial, but handsome; not with the showy finery of Paris or Vienna, but rather like a dress, whose tasteful colors and perfect adaptation to the form lead one to thoroughly admire it, without at first being able to explain its charm. An air of elegance and leisure pervades its streets. We feel that here

A STREET IN THE HAGUE.

is the repose of wealth served by attentive tradesmen. At Rotterdam, they say, one makes his fortune; at Amsterdam he increases it; but at the Hague he spends it.

One of the most impressive features of the Dutch capital is the National Monument, the sight of which recalls the founder of the nation's independence, — William, the Silent. This hero

THE PROMENADE.

is as highly revered in Holland as Washington is in the United States. As the principal opponent of Philip II. in the Netherlands, he was the incarnation of the national spirit in the noblest epoch of Dutch history, and dared to stand forth as the fearless leader of a persecuted people, in opposition to the mightiest monarch then on earth, whose kingdom included Spain, Belgium, Holland, a part of Italy, and a portion of North Africa, and threw its baneful shadow over the West Indies, Mexico, and Peru. Yet Philip II. with all these resources could

not crush him; and finally, in 1580, was base enough to offer
a reward of twenty-five thousand crowns and a title of nobility
to any one who would assassinate him. Responsive to this
shameful bribe, a score of dastardly assassins watched for a
chance to strike the fatal blow. Eight desperate attempts were
made before the one that finally succeeded. On Sunday, the
10th of July, 1584, the Prince, in company with some friends,
was going down the stairway of his house to dinner. Leaning
upon his arm was his beautiful young wife, who had already,
several years before, witnessed in Paris the murder of
her father in the massacre of St. Bartholomew. Suddenly a man stepped from a corner of the corridor
and extended a petition. The Prince requested
him to come again when he was not engaged, and
passed on to the dining- hall. The stranger
walked away without a word. During the repast, William was as usual gay and cheerful;
for his surname, "the Silent," does not im-

THE NATIONAL MONUMENT, THE HAGUE.

THE PALACE AND STATUE OF WILLIAM.

ply that he was taciturn or gloomy, but merely that he could, and did, conceal his plans with marvelous dexterity. His wife, however, appeared troubled, and spoke to him several times of the strange man whom they had just met in the hall, saying that he had certainly the most villainous face that she had ever seen. William laughed lightly at her fears and reassured her; then, at the close of the repast, he led his wife and friends once more along the corridor. As he approached the staircase, the assassin, who was waiting, sprang forth and shot him in the breast. The Prince reeled backward a few steps, and fell into the arms of his young wife. Five minutes later, one of the noblest of human hearts had ceased to beat.

Some of my pleasantest memories of the Hague are connected with the spacious park that lies between that city and the sea. Whoever is fond of level walks and drives, beneath magnificent oaks and elms, will find this park enchanting.

THE PARK.

Moreover, as it is three miles long, it is never over-crowded, and so luxuriant is its vegetation that I believe the statement made by a Dutch writer, that in the Hague and its vicinity there can be found a tree, a flower, and a bird for each of its inhabitants.

Here and there, within its cool enclosure, are villas of great beauty, in one of which the Queen resides in summer; yet there is no unusual seclusion in this abode of royalty. Strangers may wander freely through the grounds, and even enter the villa at certain hours of the day, for the park is looked upon as national property and is accessible to all. It is the remnant of an enormous forest, which formerly covered the entire territory of the Nether-lands, and en-abled its primitive

THE ROYAL VILLA.

inhabitants to resist for so long a time the legions of imperial Rome. On many of the historic elms and beeches in this forest the names of famous individuals have been bestowed. Hence they are dear to every Hollander. More than once, in their heroic struggle for independence, the Dutch were tempted to dispose of these trees for money, which was so essential; but when it came to the decisive act, the citizens always saved them by a voluntary contribution.

The history of Holland is a record of the unexpected. One would suppose that this flat country—formed principally of the mud deposited by the Rhine, the Meuse, and the Schelde — would be the last part of the world to be the scene of bloody wars and fiendish cruelties; yet on this marshy soil, threaded by sluggish streams and brooded over by the exhalations of a threatening sea, bloodshed and torture

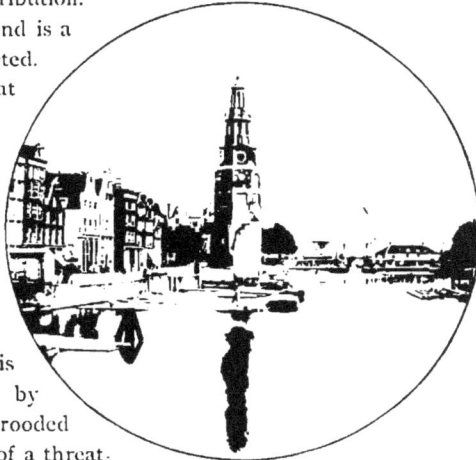

THE TOWER OF MONT ALBAN.

cast their baneful shadows for a hundred years. Here, in the sixteenth and seventeenth centuries, were enacted some of the most important deeds in the world's history; and on a land, whose very existence is a perpetual conflict between life and death, occurred a struggle for religious and political freedom, unsurpassed in suffering and heroism. The Dutch are sometimes ridiculed as being stupid. It is a serious mistake. Although they live of necessity a great part of the time in cloudland, they are the most practical people on the face of the earth. Slow they undoubtedly are; but they exemplify the fable of

the tortoise and the hare, and retain abundant proofs of their
career of conquest and commercial enterprise when they were
rivals of Great Britain, and wrested from the Portuguese the
sovereignty of the eastern seas.   Small as their mother country
is, the Dutch possess, to-day, in the Indian Ocean a splendid
archipelago, which a Holland writer has compared to a girdle
of emeralds strung along the equator; and in Java, Sumatra,
Borneo, New Guinea, and other islands they have a colonial
empire that covers an area of eight hundred thousand square
miles, and includes a population of thirty-three million souls.

After driving for two miles through the charming forest near
the Hague, we reached the little town of Scheveningen.   Historically, this is interesting as the port from which Charles II.
sailed for England when he was recalled from exile after the
death of Cromwell; but it is chiefly famous now as the fashionable watering-place of the Hague.   Between the capital and

AT SCHEVENINGEN.

ON THE BEACH.

this resort horse-cars and cabs are
always rolling back and forth; and on bright
summer days the entire population of the Hague appears to
have assembled on the ocean sands. The fashionable life
of Scheveningen is similar to that of every Continental
bathing-place. There are, of course, the grand hotels, the
crowds upon the beach, the bathing-carts, the wicker chairs
for invalids, the music, dancing, and flirtation that characterize
Brighton, Margate, Biarritz, and Ostend; but there is also
quite another life at Scheveningen, peculiar to the country, and
indicated most appropriately by the curious figures which now
and then stand forth in striking contrast to the ephemeral
gaiety on the shore. The pleasure seekers lead a butterfly
existence here for two or three months, and then depart; but
the old fishermen remain permanent features of the landscape.
I found the natives of the Holland coast interesting objects of

study.   Living within two miles of the capital, and every summer visited by the crowds of fashion, they nevertheless preserve
unchanged the primitive habits of their forefathers.   Such as
they were three centuries ago they are to-day.   The personal
appearance of some of them is extraordinary.   Their skin resembles the exterior of a smoke-cured ham, and is as thickly
seamed with wrinkles as Holland is with canals.   I fancied that

FISHERMEN'S HOUSES.

the rain must run in regular
channels down their cheeks.   Their
mouths are usually large, and, when no
teeth are visible, as is not infrequently the case, they open
like old-fashioned carpetbags.   I recollect that one of these
"toilers of the sea" had legs, the curving lines of which I
never saw surpassed, save in a wishbone or a lobster's claws;
and I could never understand what must have happened to
him in infancy to give his limbs a shape that would have made
his fortune in a dime museum.

INTERIOR OF A DUTCH COTTAGE.

The Sunday costume of the Scheveningen men consists of high-buttoned jackets, baggy trousers, and long stockings. That of the women is still more peculiar. They wear a kind of nightcap, with embroidered edges, drawn tightly over the head and ears. Beneath this hangs, on each side of the face, something which looks in the distance like a misplaced switch, but proves to be a solitary curl. The uninitiated visitor might suppose that the

A FISHERMAN.

special glory of their dress was a kind of vest, embroidered with all the colors of the rainbow; but their real wealth is estimated, not by the richness of their jackets, but by the number of skirts worn at one time. Sometimes a woman boasts of wearing twelve or fifteen, at once, fastened around her ample waist.

A SCHEVENINGEN FAMILY.

INTERIOR OF A FISHERMAN'S HOUSE.

Both men and women encase their feet in wooden shoes, which seem appropriate when half immersed in sand; but on city pavements they make a noise resembling the rattle of "bones" between the fingers of a negro minstrel.

The faces of these fisher folk look old and anxious; but who can be surprised at this? What a toilsome, cheerless life they lead the greater part of the year, when only the women and children can remain to watch and wait and keep the hearthstone bright, while all the stalwart men of the village are at sea! But when the fleet comes back there is joy indeed. Women and children then rush down upon the sands to welcome their returning fathers, husbands, and brothers. An old man rides on horseback through the surf, catches the rope thrown from the prow of the first ship, and brings back to the crowd the news as to the draught of herring, and (more important still) whether all the men are safe and well. Then follow the excitement of the landing, the eager welcome home, and, last of all, the public sale of fish upon the shore. During these scenes the sad-eyed, anxious women seem transfigured. I saw some faces which looked almost beautiful, when turned with love and pride toward the brave men who, doubtless, seemed to them like warriors coming home from battle. Nor is this strange, for as I walked along this beach, and watched the square-built, clumsy ships, I wondered that their crews ever came back from the fierce conflict with the elements. What an experience it must be to live for months, tossed up and down in rolling tubs like these, upon the billows of the terrible North Sea, which either sulks for weeks at a time beneath its sombre sky and cloak of fog, or grows tempestuous if ruffled by the lightest gale, and is forever peopled in the popular mind with monsters longing to engulf all who dare to spread a sail above its waves.

As evening deepened into night, I walked alone upon the beach at Scheveningen. A storm had swept the sea for hours, and now its cumulative waves, baffled in search of

THE BOATS.

ON THE SANDS.

other prey, sought to expend their fury on the helpless shore; but held back by the curb which Nature's tidal forces had silently imposed upon them, the angry billows spat their hatred impotently on the land in hissing spray, which rose to an appalling height and then leaped toward the beach, like some chained monster, foaming at the mouth, whose leash might break at any moment. As I surveyed it, with that mingled dread and fascination which such scenes inspire, and recollected that large portions of the land behind me lay many feet below the ocean level, the wealth and comfort I had seen in Holland's prosperous cities and

UTILIZING THE WIND.

THE RIVER AMSTEL.

productive farms appeared almost miraculous, since they had
been acquired and were preserved only by splendid courage
and untiring toil, in battling against that element which
reigns supreme over three-quarters of the globe. Eternal
vigilance is for the Dutch the price of their existence, and
watchmen must be stationed day and night upon the dikes
to give immediate warning of   approaching
peril. Moreover, a corps of engi-   neers is employed exclusively in superintend-   ing this Ti-

HOLLAND BELOW THE OCEAN LEVEL

tanic struggle ; and although more
than fifteen hundred million dollars
have been expended in constructing ramparts, two millions are
used annually to maintain them. Surely, no Hollander should
find it difficult to believe the story of the Deluge, or fail to comprehend that part of the Mosaic account of the Creation which
tells of the dividing of "the waters from the waters." Two hundred years ago Holland was described as

> "A country that draws fifty feet of water,
> In which men live as in the hold of nature ;
> And when the sea does in upon them break,
> And drowns a province, does but spring a leak."

To me, however, it resembles rather a beleaguered fortress, before whose gates a tireless foe is constantly at work, now undermining secretly its massive dikes, now charging furiously on the rescued soil, as if determined to reclaim its own. The

HOLLAND'S TIRELESS ALLY.

danger can be best appreciated by standing behind one of Holland's ocean bulwarks at high tide, and hearing the breakers dash against the other side of the wall, sixteen or eighteen feet above the level of the land. For, although calm and beautiful at times, the North Sea can be treacherous and cruel. Again and again it has forced an entrance here, and by a sudden onset of its waves has laid waste prosperous towns and peaceful villages and swept to destruction thousands of inhabitants.

In the fearful inundation, of 1570, nearly all the dikes were destroyed, ships were carried into the interior of the country, and one hundred thousand people are said to have perished. Yet the indomitable Dutch have always rallied, undismayed, to expel the foe,

ROTTERDAM HARBOR.

and have invariably succeeded. Recently, they have even assumed the offensive, and compelled the ocean to retire from land which it had occupied for centuries. Hundreds of square miles of territory have, in the last few years, been wrested from the sea solely by means of windmills; and the fields, thus rescued and walled in with massive dikes, are spotted now with herds of cattle ruminating peacefully where, but a little while ago, the sea rolled fathoms deep. Truly, a country that can thus repel an enemy of such tremendous power; and has, moreover, called the winds of heaven to assist her in the conflict, is a magnificent proof of man's superiority over nature; and, as I trod the battle-ground of these contending forces, I realized, as never before, the truth of the familiar proverb: "God made the sea, but the Dutch have made the shore."

MEXICO

MEXICO

THE oldest gateways of our great republic face the
rising sun. Through these our ancestors entered the
New World. Up to their portals for two hundred
years has swept a ceaseless flood of immigration from an
older shore. Through them, to-day, there ebbs and flows a
mighty tide of tourists, who every spring go forth to wander
in historic Europe, and every fall return through the same
gateways to their homes. Within the last few years, however,
a portion of
this stream of
travel has
sought other
channels, and
through the
doorways of
our western
coast, facing
the mightiest
ocean on our
globe, increas-
ing thou-
sands annual-
ly make their
way to Alaska
or Japan.

OUR PRIVATE CAR.

AN ADOBE HOUSE.

But transit through the ports of the Atlantic or Pacific implies an ocean voyage, which is to many a serious drawback. There still remains, however, on our southern boundary, a door which has not this objection; for there, divided from us by no ocean barrier, but only by a narrow river called the Rio Grande, lies outstretched beneath the Southern Cross, and not unlike a mighty cornucopia in form, a land of which we know as yet far less than we have learned of Europe, and hardly more than we now know of China and Japan; a country of mysterious origin and vast antiquity; of noble scenery and impressive history; of picturesque costumes, and a life half Spanish and half Oriental; the dwelling-place of Aztecs and of Spaniards; the battle-ground of

Montezuma and of Cortez; the realm of sunshine and of
silver, — Mexico.

It was exactly midnight when we glided through the southern gateway known as "Eagle Pass," and our long line of cars
crept out in Indian file upon the bridge that spans the Rio
Grande.   Below me I could see a silver streak, sharply defined
between two parallel lines, which I well knew to be the opposite
shores of the United States and Mexico.   No matter how ex-
tensively one may have traveled, he feels instinctively a thrill
of emotion
on entering
an unknown
land.   In go-
ing to Eu-
rope, this
feeling comes
upon one
gradually.
The ocean
voyage is a
preparation
for an advent
on a foreign
shore.   Enter-
ing Mexico,

AN OX-TEAM.

however, the change is almost instantaneous, and I shall
long recall the sensation I experienced, when, poised above
the Rio Grande, I saw at the same instant, in the gloom of
night, on one side the dim outline of my native land, and on
the other the sombre profile of the Mexican republic.

The next morning I awoke to find myself in a foreign
country.   I saw that we were rolling through a perfectly flat
plain, flanked on the east and west by mountain ranges.
Apparently this area was once the bed of a gigantic lake,

perhaps a portion of the Gulf of Mexico. To-day it is almost as sterile as a desert. Mile after mile, and hour after hour, we looked upon a desolate expanse of sand, arid and blistered by a burning sun. For nine months it had received no rain. Its only vegetation was a stunted growth of prickly pear and cactus plants, occasionally varied by "Spanish bayonet" trees, which look like porcupines on poles. While traveling through this dreary waste we saw, for hours at a time, no signs of life save an occasional buzzard circling in the air, in search of some poor creature stricken by the sun. In certain localities, however, goats are as numerous as on the heights above New York. Their diet is not —confined to such dyspeptic articles as sardine boxes and tomato cans; but each to his taste! To Mexican goats the Spanish bayonet spikes are doubtless just as sweet as New York clothes-pins, and prickly cactus leaves replace for them the worn-out hair brushes of Harlem.

CACTUS.

Looking upon such cheerless scenery, the traveler at first exclaims, "This is an uninviting route by which to enter Mexico"; and, it must be confessed, the first appearance of the country is exceedingly unattractive. To ride four hun-

LAGOS.

CROSSING THE DESERT.

dred miles
through alkali
plains, the
dust of which
sifts through
the windows
of the car and
lies in spoon-
fuls on his
clothing, is a
grim penalty
that every
tourist who
goes to Mex-
ico must pay.

But, after all, he has to endure it only twenty-four hours;
and what is that compared to the tribute which old Neptune
frequently exacts from travelers crossing the Atlantic? The
mountains which enclose this wilderness relieve the landscape
from complete monotony.   Their strange forms offer infinite
variety.   Without a single break, they line the desert all day
long; at times advancing, then retreating, precisely like the

rugged shores
of an extensive
lake.   When
close at hand,
their sunburnt
peaks look
savage and
forbidding;
but, at a dis-
tance, a soft,
mellow haze
conceals their

harsher features, and renders them as delicate in coloring as
an aquarelle.

We could not understand, at first, why railway stations
should have been built upon this Mexican desert. The depot
was often the only building visible, surrounded by half a dozen
scrawny palms, resembling worn-out feather dusters, and dominated by a telegraph pole, cutting its form like a gigantic
gibbet against the sky; but, several miles distant from these

A FEATHER DUSTER STATION.

stations, there is usually a large
plantation, or a little town, between which and the railroad
regular communication is main-
tained by means of tram-cars or a stage-coach. One of those
stage-coaches I shall never forget. I looked at it as I might
have gazed upon an instrument of torture used by the Inquisition. It seemed more perfectly adapted to inflict excru-
ciating misery upon its occupants than any vehicle I had ever
seen, even in the remotest districts of old Spain. Could it be
possible that after five or six decades of active service n the
Mother Country, this coach had been sent out to Mexico? Its
springs had originally been of leather, but were now of rope.
The doors had, apparently, passed through several desperate

conflicts with banditti. The windows had been long since broken out. The white dust lay so thick upon the seats that I at first supposed them to be covered with gray cloth, until I felt my fingers sink into the powdery mass to reach at last a species of bed-rock, which at some unknown period of the past had been a leather cushion. Yet this was the regular coach between the station

THE STAGE-COACH.

and a village forty miles away. Five reckless passengers were about to risk their lives in its interior. The fare was three dollars. I asked if this included the services of an undertaker on arriving at their destination, but could not get a satisfactory reply. After long years of traveling in such vehicles as this, it

SOLDIERS AT STATION.

is not strange that the Mexicans regarded tram-cars, drawn by mules along smooth rails, a priceless luxury, and made no serious objection when the railroads only came within a few miles of their towns.

A MEXICAN PRIVATE CARRIAGE.

Indeed, tramways in Mexico sometimes connect the railroad with cities thirty or forty miles distant, the longest line — between Vera Cruz and Jalapa - covering a distance of seventy-six miles. Until comparatively recent times, with the exception of the highway built from the coast by Cortez, communication here was chiefly made on horseback. The difficulties of stage-coach traveling were sometimes almost insurmountable. A Mexican gentleman told me that, twenty years ago, a trip from Guadalajara to the capital required (when the roads were good) about six days. "And how long when the roads were bad?" I asked. "Six months," was the reply.

Near one of the stations

A MEXICAN HORSEMAN.

we beheld a group of Mexican horsemen, each thoroughly armed, and wearing on his head a dark sombrero. These cavaliers were once highwaymen, who held up the stages, robbed the passengers, and rendered traveling here romantic. But President Diaz reformed them. On coming into power, he sent for their leaders and inquired: " My friends, how much does highway robbery pay you on an average every year?" They named a certain sum. " Well," continued the President, " would you not prefer to earn that money honestly and feel that you will die like Christians?" Most of them thought they would, and the interview closed with a promise of a salary of forty dollars a month; in return for which the men agreed to furnish arms and horses, and (as the "Mexican Rural Guards ") to keep the country free from bandits. With such protectors who can feel unsafe in Mexico?

PRIMITIVE LOCOMOTION.

ON THE TABLE-LAND.

The next morning, we found that we had left the desert and its heat behind and below us. All through the night our engine had been toiling upward, till we had reached the Mexican table-land.

Three-fourths of Mexico is a plateau, from six thousand to eight thousand feet above the level of the sea. Were it not lifted thus to a plane far higher than the summit of Mount Washington, the climate of Mexico would be that of Nubia; but, once transported to that height, the traveler finds a temperature delightful throughout the entire year. Unaware of this fact, I had supposed a trip to Mexico, in any season except winter, would be uncomfortable; but, on the contrary, in some respects the pleasantest time to

A MEXICAN VILLAGE.

IN THE TROPICS.

visit Aztec land is summer.   May is usually the hottest season
of the year, yet though I spent a portion of that month in the
City of Mexico I wore a light overcoat every evening.

The remaining fourth of Mexico, which is not table-land, is
easily described.   Whether the tourist journeys east or west
from the centre of the country, he will soon find himself upon
the edge of the plateau, almost as if he were standing on the
brink of a precipice.   From this the land descends abruptly,
on one side toward the Gulf
of Mexico, and on the
other toward the Pacific
and the Gulf of Cali-
fornia.   There are,
however,   certain
intervening   ter-
races,   breaking
the   steep   de-
scent, which are
called   temperate
regions,   because
the   elevation of
three thousand
feet above the sea
gives them a mod-
erate and delight-

IN THE LOWLANDS.

ful climate.   Below these are the Tierras Calientes, or Hot
Lands, of the coast.   What an amazing country then, is this,
which has three zones: the tropical, the temperate, and the
cold, ranged not from south to north, as elsewhere in the northern hemisphere, but upward, from the ocean level toward the
sky!   Moreover, on the grand plateau, some of the loftiest
mountains of our planet tower still further heavenward, wearing
eternally their coronets of snow.   In twenty-four hours, therefore, if he will, the traveler in Mexico may pass through almost

every grade of climate known upon the globe, from torrid heat
to glacial cold.

During the day, and frequently half the night, when we
were side-tracked in one place, men, women, and children
gathered about our car like sea-gulls round an ocean steamer,
eagerly seizing all the refuse thrown out by our cook, and eating
it with evident delight.   There was, however, nothing bold or

GROUP BY THE RAILROAD.

disagreeable in their sad persistency.   It was the desperate
appeal of hopeless poverty; and it was with pity, not dis-
gust, that I beheld these natives.

The finest painting that I saw in Mexico portrays an Aztec
woman, in the time of Cortez, kneeling beside the body of her
murdered husband, and appealing to a priest to save her from
the fury of the conquering Spaniards.   The scene, alas! is true
to history.   The Spaniards are responsible for what the Mexican Indians are to-day.   The Aztec race was in many ways

POLICE AND PRISONERS.

remarkably accomplished and intelligent. Their Spanish conquerors, however, mad with lust for gold, slaughtered them by thousands, and made the survivors, virtually, slaves. The Indians of to-day are, therefore, timid and retiring in manner, with a sad expression, as though they realized that they are now a crushed and conquered race. Are they susceptible of improvement? Undoubtedly. President Juarez — the ablest man whom Mexico has ever produced, the conqueror of Maximilian, and the architect of the republic — was a full-blooded Indian, a noble specimen of the old Aztec race.

I was surprised to learn how large a proportion of the present Mexican population is composed of descendants of the Aztecs. At least two-thirds of the inhabitants of Mexico are Indians, most of them poor, ignorant, and ragged. Even in the capital the proportion is about the same. I doubt not that a brilliant future is awaiting Mexico, thanks to the excellent government of President Diaz, the introduc-

A MEXICAN WATER-CART.

tion of railroads, and the development of her magnificent mineral and agricultural enterprises; but there can be no question that she has before her an Herculean task in educating seven million ignorant Indians, and elevating them to decent life and the responsibilities of citizenship.

Our first real halting-place in Mexico was Zacatecas, one of the loftiest situations on the table-land, and we saw without

ZACATECAS.

regret the train move on and leave our special car upon a side-track till the following day. The view of Zacatecas from the railroad is impressive. Directly opposite the station rises a rugged mountain, wearing, as a unique and ever to be remembered ornament, a curving

crown of perpendicular rocks, whose moss-like vegetation makes
them look like malachite. Below this I beheld what seemed to be
an Oriental city, since almost all the buildings had flat roofs, with
walls of unbaked bricks, just as one sees them in the Holy Land.

The most remarkable feature of Zacatecas is its
vivid coloring. Its varied hues are charming, and

STREET VIEW, ZACATECAS.

here an artist would be transported with delight. All the plastered
walls are painted, and every street is, therefore, framed in red,
orange, yellow, green, blue, or violet, adorned with gaily decorated
signs. Many of the buildings, it is true, are dirty and dilapidated,
and most of them have but one story. To scrutinize them closely
is disenchanting; but, in the brilliant sunshine of the tropics
and under the intense blue sky of Mexico, even squalid structures become picturesque. When I glanced down the streets, I
usually saw a multitude of motionless or moving figures, their
garments of white cotton half concealed by yellow, red, and

PLAZA FOUNTAIN, ZACATECAS.

purple blankets; and as I watched the multicolored groups,
meeting and separating, or coming and going before the
brightly tinted walls, I felt as if I were looking into a kaleido-
scope. But, while the natives are attractive at a distance, a
closer scrutiny reveals the fact that, "'Tis distance lends enchantment" to the Mexican. The peakèd hat of straw or felt
becomes, on near approach, a thing to be studied under a mi-
croscope; the bronzed face, looking in the distance so effective,
is painfully innocent of soap and water; and it would be ad-
visable to treat the brightly colored blanket as the Priest and
Levite did the traveler on the way to Jericho, when they
"passed by on the other side." As for the natives' shirts and
trousers, they call to mind the sails of an old ship, snow-white,
when seen upon the verge of the horizon, but proving upon

closer inspection to be a gray and melancholy waste of soiled
canvas, seamed with patches. It is not, I am sure, an exag-
geration to say that one-half of the inhabitants of Mexico are
either barefooted or wear a kind of sandal, consisting of a piece
of leather strapped to the foot like a skate.

We saw a number of water-venders in Zacatecas, whose
little tanks (strapped on their shoulders after the fashion of
Italian organ-grinders), contained the drinking water which
they were carrying to the houses; for water here is precious,
and has been sold sometimes as high as two cents a gallon.
If drinking water be thus scarce, it is painful to reflect on the
bathing conveniences in this Mexican city. So far as my observation went, however, the lack of water for that purpose
occasioned its inhabitants no uneasiness, — apparently to

WATER-VENDERS.

none of the natives was a bath either a reminiscence or an aspiration.

On one occasion we left our comfortable Pullman car to test the comforts of a genuine Mexican hotel. The halting-place selected for this doubtful experiment was Silao. It was midnight when we reached it. Leaving the train, a few steps brought us to a dimly lighted building, called "The Grand Hotel." A gray-haired man in *négligé* attire surveyed us, silently, as we approached.

"*Buenas Tardes*, Señor," we exclaimed, "have you received our telegram asking for five rooms?"

"I have," was the reply, "and they are ready. When do you wish to go to them?"

"As soon as possible, Señor."

"Will you have a blanket?" asked the gray-haired man.

I looked at him in some alarm, and ventured, "Yes."

"And sheets?"

"Why,—yes."

"And a pillow-case?"

"Ye—es."

"Do your companions also want such luxuries?"

I gazed at my companions. They were speechless with astonishment. Taking their silence for consent, the gray-haired man deliberately opened the door, not of the hotel-safe, but of a wardrobe. From this he took five scarlet blankets, ten sheets, five pillow-cases, and as many towels. Then calling a half-naked Indian,

HOTEL AT SILAO.

"THE STAIRCASE."

he piled this bed-
ding on his back,
as if he were a
donkey, and bade
him lead us to
our rooms. After
one look at the
Indian, we much
preferred to carry
our own bed-
clothes ; but, be-
ing too tired to
attempt it, we
followed him up
the staircase.
This was no
easy undertaking, for the hotel corridors were in total darkness,
and as our Indian was of the color of a burnt ginger-snap, he
shed no radiance through the gloom.   Providentially, however,
though he was lost to us by the sense of sight, another of our
senses permitted
no doubt of his
locality.

We presently
found him light-
ing five candles
for as many
rooms. There was
no choice in these
apartments. Each
had two iron beds,
a lilliputian wash-
stand, two chairs,
and a scanty piece

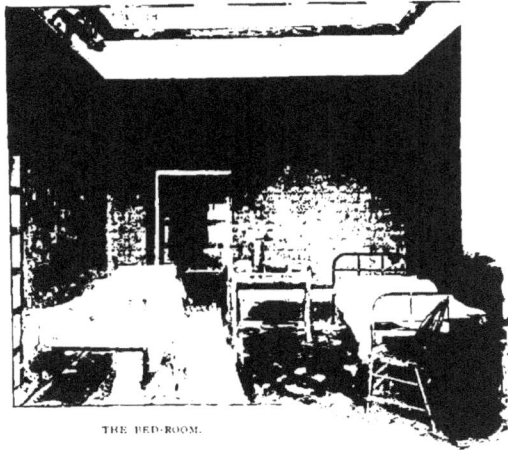

THE BED-ROOM.

of matting stuck like a postage-stamp upon a floor of stone. There were no windows, and doors in the form of blinds gave to these rooms their only light and air. The night that followed marked the greatest triumph of insomnia that my life has ever known. In the first place, my pillow was as flat and hard as an adobe brick; and, secondly, some choice Silao fleas had left the Indian bedclothes-bearer for a change of diet. Then, too, to make my misery complete, close by the Grand Hotel, a chorus of roosters was rehearsing in distracting unison. Aroused by these, a score of dogs kept barking till they gasped for breath; while, ever and anon, a melancholy donkey, worn with toil, would burst into a fit of asinine hysterics, and shared apparently my mournful vigil till the dawn.

Leaving Silao the next morning, a short and pleasant journey brought us to Guanajuato, a curious old city, famous for three hundred years. With its flat-roofed adobe houses, it is, like Zacatecas, Oriental in appearance, and is surrounded by a

A STREET, GUANAJUATO.

A STREET AND CART.

range of mountains which look as lifeless as the moon, and as devoid of value as a beggar's hand. But, in reality, these mountains are veritable treasure-houses. Their tawny frames are interlaced with countless veins of silver, whose life-blood stirs the pulse of the financial world. The mines of Guanajuato are ranked among the richest on our planet, and they have given to the world a very large amount of its existing stock of silver. The visitor does not, however, see much evidence of wealth in Guanajuato's streets. Most of the buildings are as plain as though the neighboring hills were merely heaps of sand, the pavements are hardly more comfortable to walk on than the beds of dried-up mountain brooks, and

COURTYARD OF A MEXICAN HOUSE.

STREET IN GUANAJUATO.

the poor natives seem in want not only of silver, but of clothing. Yet, Guanajuato is a picturesque old town. Built on two sides of a ravine, its houses hang upon the cliffs, as if they had been blown into the air by some reckless blast, and had alighted by good fortune on convenient ledges. A hasty traveler would probably consider Guanajuato very unattractive as a place of residence, and might suppose its only inhabitants were poverty-stricken Indians; but a Mexican gentleman assured me that he would rather live here than anywhere else in Mexico, except the capital. "Why so?" I asked. "Because," was the reply, "the society of the town is delightful. Nowhere have I more charming friends than in Guanajuato."

WASHING TAILINGS.

We visited here one of the establishments where silver is extracted from the ore. Its high walls gave it the appearance of a feudal castle. Close by were some Indians, mining on their own account; for, even in the refuse of the mill, sufficient silver can be found to repay a native for his toil. Formerly no attention was bestowed upon such clay, and bricks were made from it for building purposes. To-day, however, it is known

that there may be more silver in a single house wall than the entire structure is worth as a residence. Entering the mill, we found ourselves in a long, poorly lighted hall, filled with appliances apparently left over from the sixteenth cen-

THE MILL.

tury. Each side was lined with shallow bowls half-filled with water. In these a certain amount of ore is placed, together with copper and sulphate of iron; and through the semi-liquid mass large stones are dragged for hours, by wretched mules, until the ore becomes a pasty mixture looking like black mud. This is then taken to an open courtyard where quicksilver and other ingredients are added. To mix these elements thoroughly, mules are made to tramp through it, back and forth, for about thirty days, until the filthy mass is ready to be washed, strained, and

COURT OF THE MILL.

smelted. Experts declare that twenty per cent. of the precious metal is wasted by these primitive processes, and that with proper machinery the work could be far better done in a hundredth part of the time. But, even with present appliances, the profits are so large that there is little incentive for improvement.

Before I left the place, I had the curiosity to examine one of the mules, which had for months been tramping through the mixture. It was a pitiable sight. Its color was a ghastly green, its eyes were nearly closed, exposure to the mineral mass had burned the hair and some of the flesh from feet and legs, and thoroughly poisoned its whole system. I do not know of any animals in the world more worthy of pity than the mules of Guanajuato. Omnibus horses lead a life of luxury

THE SICK MULE.

and ease compared with them. Not only do these mules have
to drag, blindfolded, for many years their heavy burdens in the
treadmills; but, finally, when old and helpless they come into
this courtyard to be killed gradually by the mineral poison,
which causes them to assume meantime the varied hues of
the chameleon.

The Citadel of Guanajuato
(now used as a prison) has played
a prominent
part in Mexican
history. Dur-
ing Mexico's
war for inde-
pendence, in
1810, by which
she sought to
free herself
from Spanish
tyranny, Gua-
najuato was the
heart of the re-
bellion and the
scene of its

THE CITADEL.

most desperate struggles. Here the brave patriot-priest Hidalgo
(in some respects the Washington of Mexico), having raised the
standard of revolt against the Mother Country, gave battle to the
Spanish army and defeated it. It is true, this victory was soon
avenged, and eleven years rolled by before Hidalgo's dream of
Mexican freedom could come to pass; but finally it was realized,
notwithstanding the heroic patriot had meantime perished in the
strife, and though upon a corner of this citadel his head had
been displayed as a ghastly trophy, in the vain hope of striking
his compatriots with fear.

While walking through the streets of Guanajuato, I saw

an Indian going from house to house, and offering for sale a coffin! We sometimes think that the Mexicans have no enterprise; but, really, for an undertaker to send out drummers to solicit trade was a little beyond anything I had ever met before. This incident had a remarkable effect upon our guide.

"That reminds me," he cried, "we must now ascend the hill to the cemetery."

"Climb to a graveyard?" exclaimed one member of our party scornfully, "not I, it is too hard work."

THE COFFIN-PEDDLER.

"My friend," replied the guide, "fear nothing. You shall be wafted there, as if upon a cloud. We are to ride on burros."

He vanished, and a few minutes later the promised donkeys came in sight. They had a melancholy look, as if repeated visits to the graveyard depressed their spirits. All of them had rough, unkempt hair, and on their backs had been placed bags of corn-husks, as substitutes for saddles. One donkey was distinguished from the rest by having a piece of rope for a bridle, but the others were supposed to be guided merely by the rider's kicks. So huge, however, were the corn-husk saddles that when we mounted them our limbs looked like the blades of a tailor's shears stretched to their full extent, and not a heel could possibly approach the body of the beast

DONKEY RIDING.

below. Thus seated, like distended jumping-jacks, we rode with shouts of laughter up the hill, and reached at last a hollow square entirely open to the sky. The walls surrounding it, which have a thickness of eight feet, were honeycombed with pigeonholes like letter-boxes in a post-office. In these receptacles the dead of Guanajuato are left, as books are placed on shelves, one tier above another, and when a space is filled with a coffin, the opening is closed with a marble slab that serves

not only for a door, but also for a tombstone. Some of these pigeonholes are bought outright for a hundred dollars, but the greater number are merely rented for five years. When the time expires, the bones

THE CEMETERY.

AN OLD GRAVE-DIGGER.

are taken out, and the space is swept and garnished for the next comer, like a berth in a sleeping-car.

"What becomes of the evicted tenants?" I inquired.

"Look there and see," was the reply.

I turned, and saw two well-nigh naked grave-diggers tossing up skulls and bones from a trench in the enclosure.

"At first," explained the guide, "the bodies taken from the walls are buried here; but even this is only for a little time. Five acres do not constitute a cemetery large enough for Guanajuato; hence, the first occupants must soon resign their places to others."

"What is then their destination?" I asked.

"They go down to the cata-combs," he answered; "would you like to see them?"

WAITING FOR AN ENGAGEMENT.

I hesitated. " I will go down," exclaimed the photographer, " I wish to see if there is light enough there for making illustrations."

Accordingly he disappeared. A moment later, we heard a cry of horror, and soon beheld his face emerge from the ground, white as a sheet, and with distended eyes.

" Look here," he said, " I don't want to stay down there alone. You must all keep me company."

"What is it?" we demanded.

"It is indescribable," murmured the artist, " go down and see."

Thus urged, we made our way down twenty steps and entered a long corridor. There

THE CRYPT.

was a general exclamation of astonishment. Before us was a crypt about twenty feet in height and one thousand feet in length. For centuries it has served as the receptacle of bones discarded from the court above, till almost the entire space is now filled to the roof with skulls, legs, arms, ribs, hip-joints, and shoulder-blades heaped up from floor to ceiling, like corn-cobs in a granary. Moreover, in the immediate foreground, thirty or forty mummies have been placed upright against the wall, and look like ghastly sentinels guarding the chaotic mass of their companions.

The most useful plant in Mexico is the Maguey. "It is a cactus," I exclaimed, when I first beheld it.

"It does belong to the cactus family," was the reply, "and closely resembles what you call the Century Plant. In Mexico, however, it is not allowed to bloom; but, on the contrary, at flowering time the Mexicans cut into its nucleus or heart. The cavity thus formed is filled at once with a rich, liquid sap, which is a source of enormous profit to the owner. At this stage of the plant's development a native comes to it several times a day to do the milking."

"What do you mean by 'milking' a plant?" I asked in some amusement.

"I refer to the extraction of its sap," was the reply, "and if you watch yonder native, you will see how it is done." I turned, and saw an Indian thrust the point of a hollow tube into the cavity of the plant, and suck the other end with all his might. His powers of persuasion in that line were certainly remarkable, for the sap, yielding to the suction, immediately filled the tube which the Indian quickly emptied into a pig-skin carried on his back. "This does not seem to me very appetizing," I said, "but it is interesting. What next is done with it?"

MILKING THE MAGUEY.

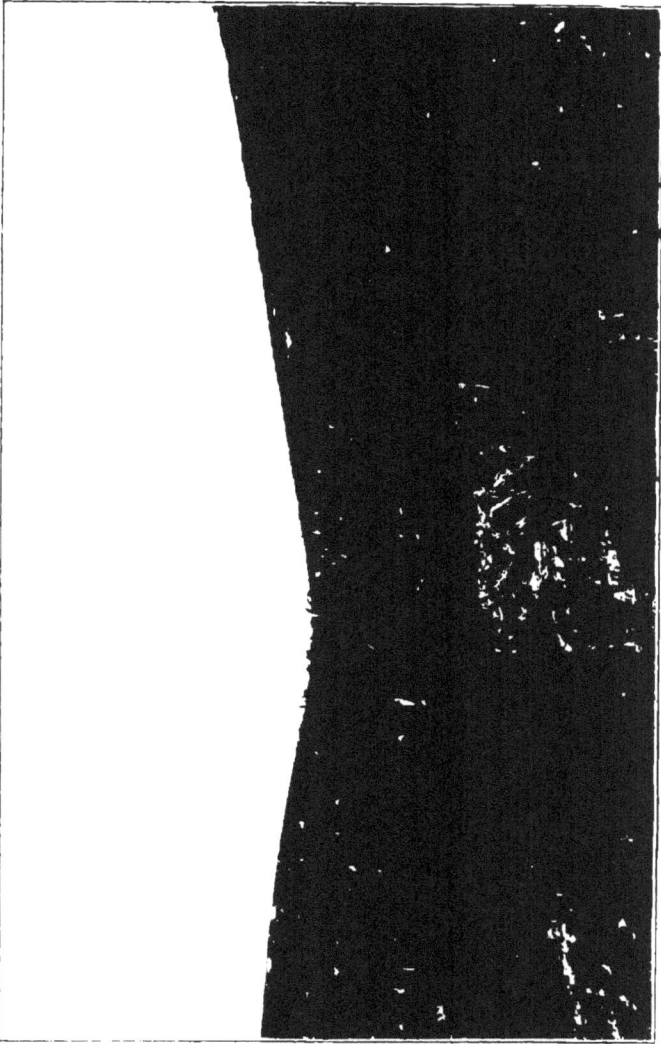

A MACCEY FARM.

"Look over there upon the road," he rejoined; "that cart, the mules of which are raising such a dust, is loaded with pig-skins full of sap. They are to be taken to the farm, and emptied into vats, in which the liquid will ferment for twenty-four hours, till it becomes *pulque* (a magic word in the republic), when it is sent away to be immediately sold."

"Why 'immediately'?" I inquired, "can it not be bottled up and kept like lager beer?"

"Impossible," said my companion. "It will not remain sweet more than forty-eight hours. Moreover, the least adverse ingredient will ruin it. An overseer, who had been discharged by his employer, once revenged himself by

CARTING PULQUE TO MARKET.

throwing a few drops of acid into his master's vat of pulque, thus spoiling what was worth a thousand dollars."

We climbed a little elevation and gazed upon the farm. It was a pretty sight. For many miles the fields looked like gigantic carpets of a terra-cotta groundwork, with the huge plants as decorative figures on their surfaces.

"How much time does the maguey require to ripen sufficiently to give forth sap?" I asked.

"About seven years," was the response. Even on reaching maturity, it furnishes the precious liquid for only about six weeks, and then dies; but, since another is immediately planted in its place, there is a constant series of arrivals and departures

A RICH FIELD.

of maguey plants on these farms, like successive classes graduating from, and entering, a public school.

The owner of a pulque farm is usually wealthy; for the maguey crop can be counted on with absolute certainty. No insects spoil it, no weather affects it, and it can be made to yield the whole year round. Best of all, the liquid is at once disposed of at a good price and for ready cash. I gained some conception of the extent of the business, when I was told that from this district a long train, loaded with nothing but pulque, goes to the City of Mexico every morning throughout the entire year; and that for running this train alone the Vera Cruz railroad is paid thirty thousand dollars a month, or a thousand dollars a day. One man in the City of Mexico owns sixty shops, and sells twelve hundred dollars' worth of pulque daily. He is supposed to make a profit of sixty

thousand dollars a year. A Mexican gentleman told me that his father owned a plantation of about ninety thousand maguey plants, one-tenth of which reach maturity every year. From this "small" plantation he receives an income of ten thousand dollars annually.

"Why does not every one go into the pulque business?" I asked.

"More would undoubtedly do so," was the answer, "but (fortunately, or unfortunately), the district where good pulque can be produced is limited to a small area, and hence the farmers in that region have a monopoly."

Personally, there are few things of which I am so certain as the fact that I would infinitely rather be a producer of pulque than a consumer. I

SELLING PULQUE AT THE RAILWAY STATION.

never shall forget the first glass of it that I tasted. An Indian Hebe offered it to me at a railway station, and I paid only a cent for it; but after one swallow, I considered a penny an exorbitant sum for what I had obtained. In color, consistency, odor, and taste Mexican pulque seemed to me like sour mucilage. People assured me that I would like it after a time. If so, it will be when "my time has come." Some travelers, however, find its taste agreeable, and the Mexicans are as fond of it as negroes are of watermelons.

On awakening, next morning, I found that we were side-tracked near an aqueduct of grand proportions. I rubbed my eyes. "Where are we?" I exclaimed, "in Rome?"

"No," was the answer, "but near one of the most interesting cities of the Mexican republic, — Querétaro, which has a population of fifty thousand, and is situated as high above the sea as the summit of Mount Washington."

"And this aqueduct?" I demanded.

"It is the work of the Spaniards," was the answer. "Built here one hundred and fifty years ago, it still brings to the town delicious water from a spring five miles away. It makes its entry over seventy-four of these arches, the highest being ninety-four feet above the ground. Expensive?" he continued, "I should say so. Its cost was about one

THE AQUEDUCT.

hundred and twenty-five thousand dollars; but of that sum eighty-three thousand were contributed by one public-spirited citizen."

Leaving our car in the shadow of the aqueduct, we drove to the neighboring city of Querétaro. Its Plaza charmed us with its wealth of palms, banana trees, and semi-tropical vegetation. It was here that Maximilian, during the siege which terminated in his death, was wont to take his evening walk. Accordingly the place recalls one of the most pathetic episodes of modern

THE PLAZA QUERETARO.

history. The coming of Maximilian to Mexico was not like that of Cortez an attempt at conquest. He came at the solicitation of a Mexican political party which he believed to be decidedly in the majority.

One day, in 1863, a dozen men-of-war from England, France, and Spain entered the harbor of Vera Cruz to obtain satisfaction for their governments. Satisfaction for what? Chiefly for financial loans which these European nations had made to Mexico, and which the Mexican authorities, declaring themselves bankrupt, had refused to pay. No wonder that poor Mexico was bankrupt. In forty years she had passed through thirty-six changes of government, and had had seventy-three presidents, —

an average of nearly two a year. Distinguished Mexican representatives were, therefore, pleading with different European powers to come to her assistance.

THE HARBOR OF VERA CRUZ.

THE FOUNTAIN, QUERÉTARO.

One of the sovereigns to whom an appeal was made was Napoleon III. There is no doubt that he and others of the crowned heads of Europe received the proposition eagerly. Our great republic was then apparently in its death agony. The time was ripe, they thought, to found an empire on the North American continent. Spain wished to give to Mexico a Bourbon Prince. To this Napoleon III. would not consent, but (willing to renounce French claims) agreed to accept an Archduke from the house of Austria, — Maximilian. He was a man of noble character and lofty principles. Within his veins flowed royal blood, distinctly traceable through six hundred years. He was accomplished, spoke six languages, and had a gentle disposition, which attracted all with whom he came in contact. This Prince, in April, 1864, having renounced his rights to the throne of Austria, sailed

MAXIMILIAN'S THRONE.

with his wife, Carlotta, for the land where they aspired to found
a new and glorious dynasty. They were both young; he was
but thirty-two, and she only twenty-four years old. The prospect was alluring. Napoleon III. had pledged his army and his
treasury to keep them on the throne; and they looked forward
to the time when Mexico, reclaimed from anarchy, would, under
their beneficent sway, assume her place among the nations of
the earth, — a close ally and *protégé* of the Old World.

THE BRIDGE

Remembering these facts, we left the Plaza of Querétaro
and approached a picturesque stone bridge upon the out-
skirts of the town. " This," said the Mexican colonel who
was our guide, "was the last point yielded by the imperial
army. When this was taken by our troops, no hope
remained for Maximilian." Napoleon III. (alarmed at the
decisive action of the United States), had heeded Secretary
Seward's warning and withdrawn his troops, and, thus

deserted, the Conservative party, which had enthusiastically
welcomed Maximilian, was now unable to withstand the Liberals under President Juarez. It was unfortunate that Maximilian remained in Mexico. He should have abdicated, and
returned to Europe with Napoleon's troops; but certain
motives, which we must admire, still detained him. Aside
from an unwillingness to give up and confess an ignomini-
ous failure, he wished, if possible, to save from vengeance
the men whose cause he had espoused and who were clinging to his fortunes. Their doom, however, like his own was
rapidly approaching. The old Convent of Querétaro, known
as La Cruz, was the last retreat and stronghold of the
Emperor. It was two o'clock in the morning when Maximilian's bosom friend and trusted officer, General Lopez,
having resolved to play the part of Judas, proceeded silently
through the dark streets to a small opening in the city
wall, where he conferred with the republican commander.
A plan of action was agreed upon, and so adroitly was it
carried out that, two hours later, Querétaro and Maximilian
were captured by the Liberals.

HOUSE WHERE MAXIMILIAN WAS CONFINED.

About a mile beyond the
city walls is a little eminence
called the Hill of the Bells. Hither,
at seven o'clock, on the morning of the 19th of June, 1867, were
brought the three distinguished prisoners who had been condemned to die, — the Emperor Maximilian and his leading generals, Miramon and Mejia. Three stone posts mark the places
where they stood. Stationed at a little distance from them were
three thousand soldiers. On arriving, Maximilian stepped from
his carriage and handed to a servant his hat and handkerchief,
which he requested should be given to his mother and brother.
Are we surprised that he left nothing for Carlotta, the wife whom
he so dearly loved? It was because he had been told (no doubt
to make his death the easier to bear) that she was dead. If he
had known the truth! In reality, poor Carlotta, who had gone
to Europe in the vain hope of gaining some assistance for her
husband, had, through her terrible anxiety and disappointment,

become hopelessly insane. At length the Emperor turned and
looked upon the seven men chosen to be his executioners. "Poor
fellows!" he murmured, "they have an unpleasant duty before
them." Then, drawing from his pocket seven twenty-dollar
gold pieces, stamped with his inscription, he gave them to the
officer in command to be presented to the soldiers when he
was no more. "My friends," he said (pointing to his breast)
"be good enough to spare my face and aim directly here."
Then, looking about him on the lovely landscape, he exclaimed:
"What a beautiful day! It is on such a day as this that I
have always wished to die."

THE SQUAD OF SOLDIERS.

The men who here awaited death were of different nation-
alities and each, unconsciously, at this impressive moment
showed the characteristics of his race. Mejia was an Indian,
and stood with the composure of a fatalist, sadly but uncom-
plainingly accepting the decree of destiny. Miramon was of
Franco-Spanish origin, and brilliant and audacious jested to the
last. The Emperor, with the well-known temperament of the
house of Austria, faced death with dignity like his ancestor,
Marie Antoinette. His first position was in the centre of the
group, but at the last moment it was changed. Miramon, who

THE HILL OF THE BELLS.

was at the Emperor's left, turning toward Maximilian had laughingly exclaimed, " You see that in this tragedy I am in the position of the impenitent thief." The Emperor answered gravely : " Permit me, then, to yield this place to you. A brave man like yourself deserves it." Thus speaking, he stepped quickly to the left, leaving Miramon in the centre ; and it was where the stone post at the extreme right stands that Maximilian fell.

Returning from this mournful spot we saw, in the governor's palace at Querétaro, the plain pine coffin in which Maximilian's body was brought back from execution. It is in places deeply stained with blood. Not long, however, did his lifeless form remain in Mexico. A few months later, by permission of the Mexican Government, the body was taken to Vera Cruz, and the same vessel which, three years before, had brought Maximilian and Carlotta to the New World in perfect health and with the brightest anticipations, took

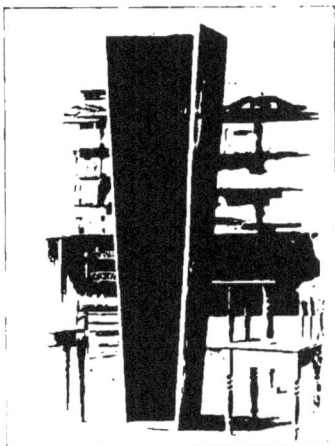

THE COFFIN.

back his mutilated form to Austria. Still more pathetic is the fact that the widowed Empress still lives, crazed with grief, a wreck upon the cruel ocean of existence.

Saying farewell to Querétaro with some reluctance, on the following evening we left the railroad at a station called El Castillo. Our purpose was to visit the Falls of Juanacatlan, sometimes enthusiastically styled the " Mexican Niagara." Upon the platform stood a gentleman who was presented to us under the euphonious name of Señor Bermejillo. His home is in the City of Mexico, but his estate at El Castillo is so vast, that, from the moment we arrived until we left, every point of land on which we stood, and almost everything we saw, was his property. In fact, he has constructed between the station and the falls a private tramway, by which in twenty minutes we reached a place where we beheld in their majestic beauty the Falls of Juanacatlan. The river Lerma (the largest stream in Mexico) here falls seventy feet in one grand mass of creamy foam, six hundred feet in breadth. Of course this cannot seriously be ranked with the stupendous volume of Niagara, yet at a glance one sees a resemblance to it. It is, in fact, Niagara in miniature, — a diamond

FALLS OF JUANACATLAN.

edition of the Horseshoe Falls; or, as it were, Niagara itself seen through the large end of an opera-glass. We stood for a long time beside this falling river, delighted with its cool, refreshing spray and its unceasing rush and roar. No doubt its beauty appealed to us with added force because of the comparative rarity of waterfalls in Mexico. What I most missed and longed for during our Mexican tour was running water, especially as only a few months before I had been traveling in Norway, which is preëminently, of all the countries of the world, the land of cataracts and cascades.

It was seven o'clock in the evening when our train arrived in the City of Mexico. A friend who had been notified of our arrival met us on the platform.

CITY OF MEXICO.

"You are in luck," he cried, "there is to be a splendid ball at the Jockey Club to-night. I have secured a ticket for you, and you must go."

"What! after ten days' constant travel?" I replied. "No, no, I am too tired." "But to-morrow you can rest." "I have not time now to get ready." "You need not go till midnight." "My dress suit is at the bottom of my trunk." "I will unpack it for you." "I do not know the way." "I will call for you in my carriage. Besides," he added, "you will have a chance to see our prettiest señoritas and our President."

THE RAILROAD STATION.

Some hours later, I found myself riding through the city. It was the hottest season of the year, yet both my comrade and myself were comfortable in light overcoats. Through the cab windows I could see block after block of buildings standing ghostlike in the silvery moonlight. Enormous windows, iron gratings, and frequently in front of them a line of donkeys driven by swarthy Indians, succeeded one another in a weird monotony. Two

STREET WITH BURROS

or three times my comrade pointed out a souvenir of history.

"Along this street," he said, "Cortez retreated

A MEXICAN CAB.

from the Aztec capital. Just here his leading general, Alvarado, made his famous leap for life, and this," he added, "was the residence of Marshal Bazaine during the French occupation under Maximilian."

"Stop a moment," I said, and leaning forward I surveyed the former dwelling of the man whose cruelties contributed so much to Maximilian's downfall, and who, on his return to France, betrayed his country by surrendering Metz to the Prussians, and, consequently, died a wretched exile in a foreign land. Nevertheless, in looking at these structures, I did not seem to realize where I was; for, though accustomed to unlooked-for incidents in travel, I had never made so strange an entry into

THE ALAMEDA.

a foreign city, when, four hours after my arrival, I drove through moonlit streets with a comparative stranger to a ball, and on the way beheld the forms of dusky Indians crouching in their blankets, and gazed on buildings dating from the days of Cortez. At last we reached the mansion of the Jockey Club, — a handsome structure covered with glazed tiles.

This singular decoration owes its origin to caprice. The Mexicans, to exemplify an almost incredible climax of extravagance, are wont to

THE JOCKEY CLUB.

say, " He never will build a house of tiles."   Some years ago,
however, one of the gilded youth of Mexico resolved to prove
that such display was not impossible, and built a house which is
enameled from roof to pavement with blue tiles.   This, when I
saw it on the night of my arrival, was gay with lights, and dif-
fused its radiance through the darkness like a porcelain lamp.

Alighting from the carriage, we entered the mansion which

COURTYARD OF JOCKEY CLUB.

was thronged with guests.   Around its spacious courtyard
tropic plants formed fragrant walls of foliage and flowers; and
over and around these banks of color floated soft music from
an unseen orchestra.   Meantime, in the rooms above, the music
of a second orchestra invited all to join in dancing, the pastime
in which Mexicans excel.

At length my comrade led me to a room apart and said,
" Allow me to present you to the honored chief of our republic,

President Diaz." I saw
before me a tall, dignified
man about fifty years of age.
Although attired in civilian's
dress, a glance would have
assured me he had been a
soldier. His manner was
extremely courteous; but I
could not forget, even amid
these fashionable surroundings, that I was in the presence of a man accustomed
to command and able to
maintain his power against
desperate odds. Porfirio

PRESIDENT DIAZ.

Diaz is not only a brave soldier, and the best ruler Mexico has
ever had; he is, besides, an able statesman, who has encouraged
the building of railroads, promoted agricultural enterprises, and
established friendly intercourse with other nations. At the same

THE PRIVATE RESIDENCE OF PRESIDENT DIAZ.

time, he has shown
wonderful ability
and tact in quiet-
ing and strength-
ening his own
land, previously
torn by frequent
revolutions. On
coming into
power, instead of
banishing or
shooting his op-
ponents, he won
them over to his
side. Thus, he

would send for a man who had been a captain in some revolutionary faction, and would say to him: " My friend, you see you are defeated. I have the power now and mean to keep it; but far from wishing to be rid of you, I need just such brave men as you to help my administration. Let us be friends. You are a captain now; henceforth, in my army, be a colonel." This shrewd, conciliatory course proved remarkably successful, and the former enemies of Diaz are now his friends.

The morning after the ball I started out with my companions to see the City of Mexico by daylight, and we drove immediately to the Plaza Mayor, or Great Square, which occupies the centre of the capital. Before us, on one side, rose the cathedral, which from a distance had appeared to be well pro-

THE CATHEDRAL.

portioned, while its fine towers had won our admiration. The site of the building is historic; for, on the spot where now its gilded crosses rise toward heaven, stood formerly the grandest temple of the Montezumas, so that the foundation of this Christian church rests on the broken images of Aztec gods. We climbed to one of its belfries and gazed upon the scene below. Directly at our feet lay the Plaza Mayor, which four hundred years ago was an open space before the Aztec temple.

This square was then the nucleus of the city's life and around it were its finest buildings. A Roman would have called it the Aztec Forum. The residence of Montezuma has been replaced, on the same site, by the National Palace, where all the different govern-

THE NATIONAL PALACE.

ments with which poor Mexico has been blessed or cursed, for centuries, have for a time had their headquarters. At present it contains the official apartments of President Diaz and many of the State Departments.

Descending from the belfry we entered the cathedral. Its grand dimensions are imposing, for the vast structure has a

THE CHAMBER OF DEPUTIES.

length of nearly four hundred feet. Formerly, too, if we can credit what the Spaniards say of it, the richness of its decoration rivaled that of any other in the world; but most of that magnificence has dis-

THE INTERIOR OF THE CATHEDRAL.

appeared, and what remains cannot atone for many serious blemishes. Thus, for a church like this to have a wooden floor is painfully incongruous; and stuccoed walls, however large, cannot command our admiration like statue-crowned and exquisitely sculptured stone. Its chapels, it is true, contain a vast amount of gilded ornamentation; but iron gratings tipped with gold-leaf are not to be compared with the elaborately carved woodwork that we see in Spain, or with the balustrades of malachite and porphyry which we find in Russia; while the majority of statues in all Mexican churches are merely plaster, colored as brilliantly as chromos.

The hotel in the City of Mexico best known to travelers was formerly the palace of the short-lived Emperor, Iturbide, whose name it bears. It looks palatial still. It has a height rarely attained by Mexican houses; electric lights suspended from the roof give to its shadowy corridors the effect of moonlight; and, most astonishing of all, an elevator (the only one in the republic in 1892) ascends serenely to the upper story. But from these brilliant externals the tourist must not expect too much from the Hotel Iturbide. Its proprietor has not fully recovered from the attack of self-esteem which the acquisition of the elevator gave him. He sits and looks at it, like a mother gazing on her first-born; and as the stewards on a certain line

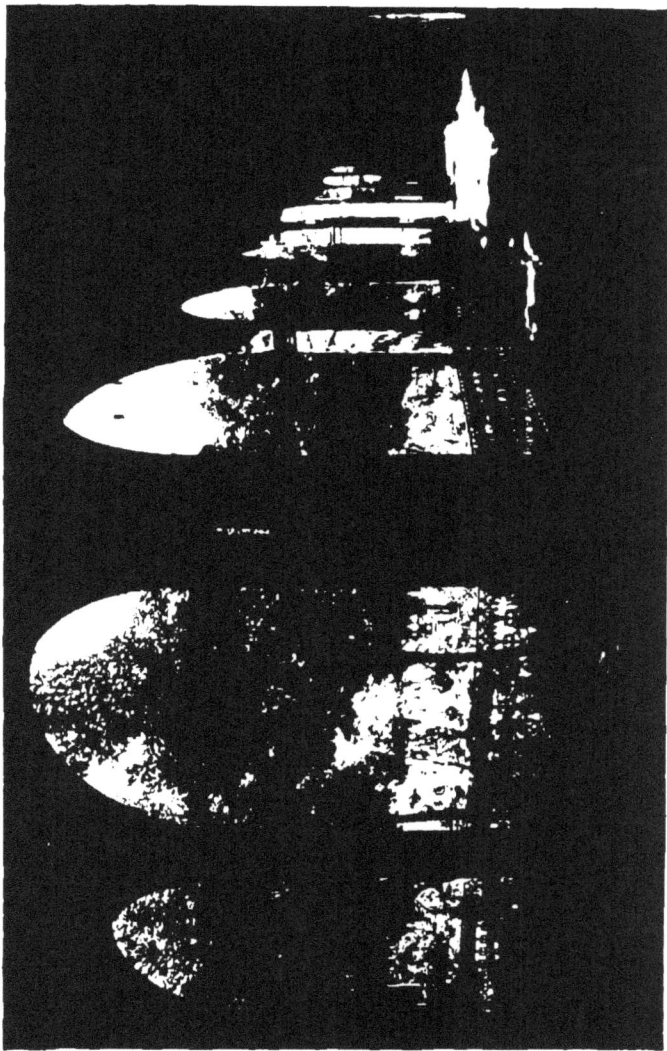

THE PATIO OF A HACIENDA.

of trans-Atlantic steamers say, "Our table is poor, but we have never lost a life," so the proprietor of the Iturbide blandly answers all complaints by proudly pointing toward his elevator, which, by the way, is allowed to run only between the hours of ten in the morning and ten at night!

The agent of an American excursion party once applied to the manager of the Iturbide for accommodations. "How much are these rooms a day?" he asked. "Four dollars each," was the reply. "But," said the agent smiling, "I shall probably bring you eighty people, how much then?" "Five dollars," said the proprietor, yawning; "that will make more trouble."

One day as I was strolling about the city, I noticed, on the upper story of a house, a bunch of newspapers tied with a string to the iron grating of a window. "What does that mean?" I asked.

"It is the recognized sign," was the reply, "that rooms are to rent there."

THE HOTEL ITURBIDE.

"What!" I exclaimed, "is it possible that, to avoid the expense of printing placards, it is the custom here to tie newspapers about a railing when one wishes to let rooms?"

"Precisely so," answered my informant, "and when a newspaper cannot be had, a bit of wrapping-paper answers the same purpose."

A MEXICAN HOUSE.

Not far from this, my companion pointed out to me another private residence, and said, "Beneath that corner window, for six months, regularly every night, I saw a faithful lover 'playing the bear.'"

"Playing the bear!" I echoed, "do you refer to the hugs which bears are wont to give their victims?"

"Oh, no!" was the reply, "the Mexican lover plays the part of Bruin in a cage. That is to say, at a fixed hour each day he saunters up and down the sidewalk near his loved one's house, gazes with rapture at her window, and puts his hand discreetly on his heart. Meantime he is being critically examined (no doubt through opera-glasses), not only by the young lady herself, but by all the other members of her family. After this dull business has dragged on for several weeks, the bear gets bold enough to write a note, and, holding it in his paw, allows his lady love to see it from a distance. That night she intercepts the servant

THE HOUSE OF THE BEAR.

and obtains it. Most probably, however, the note is read to her mamma and answered, if at all, at her dictation. At length the father appears upon the scene and makes inquiries into the habits of the bear, asking particularly how large an amount of honey he extracts from some commercial beehive! If a bear market prevails, the lover is accepted. If not, he is warned off the premises." Meanwhile, during the period of courtship, if the gratings which exclude the bear are on the lower story, the lovers are fortunate in-

A MEXICAN BALCONY

deed; for, though the advances made by Bruin are not rapid, as
an accepted suitor he is allowed to cross the street and talk with
his inamorata through the bars. There he will offer her sweet-
meats, and may sometimes hold her hand; occasionally, he will
even press it to his lips; and, possibly, if the space be wide
enough, — alas! what will not lovers do in such a case from the
days of Pyramus and Thisbe, to our own? When the bars are
on the second story, the wretched lover (forced by necessity to
be inventive) induces some kind friend to lend his shoulders as
a ladder, and even to play the guitar, so that the lady has the
double pleasure of conversing with her *fiancé* and listening to a
serenade. Sometimes, however, the serenader's back suddenly
gives way, and Romeo unceremoniously drops from heaven
to earth. Even when formally admitted to the house, the lover
sees the lady only before others, until at last the marriage cere-
mony takes place, and he secures an opportunity to test the value
of the Russian proverb: "Before going to war, pray once; before
going to sea, pray twice; before going to get married, pray
three times."

Excellent time is made on the tram-

TRAM-CARS.

ways in the City of Mexico. Some of the cars are furnished with a sign requesting passengers not to cause delay by making their farewells too long! This is, however, a necessary rule, for these affectionate people kiss repeatedly, and pat each other caressingly on the back, as they meet and part. Frequently, too, they daintily gather into a group the finger-tips of the right hand, press them an instant to the lips, and then expand them, like the opening of a tiny umbrella, blowing meantime upon the unfolding fingers as if to waft five kisses to the loved one.

Walking one day through the Mexican capital, I turned the corner of a street and stopped in astonishment at the sight before me. It was a tram-car drawn by four black horses, and adorned with wreaths of flowers and a tall black cross. Moreover, the sides were open, and on a platform in the centre a coffin was distinctly visible. This seemed to me the most extraordinary way in which to utilize a horse-car track that I had ever seen. I doubt if there is anything like it in the world, outside of Mexico; but here the tram-car com-

A FIRST-CLASS FUNERAL CAR.

A SECOND-CLASS FUNERAL CAR

panies are pre-
pared to furnish
hearses at all
prices, from richly
decorated vehicles
drawn by horses
to very plain cars
drawn by mules.
The great objec-
tion to these tram-
car funerals is not,
as might be sup-
posed, their lack
of privacy (for
the blinds and
doors of the cars can be tightly closed), but the rapidity with
which the funeral trains are run in order to clear the tracks for
regular traffic.   In the cheaper grades of funerals the small
black mules are driven wildly through the streets, and they rush

around the corners at
full gallop, presenting
an astonishing combi-
nation of "the quick
and the dead."

One of the most
interesting buildings
in the city is the Na-
tional Museum, which
contains valuable rel-
ics of the Aztec race.
The first of these
to attract my notice
was a circular mono-
lith of porphyry, three

feet thick, twelve feet in height, and weighing twenty-six tons. Inscriptions prove that this was brought from the quarry to the Aztec capital four hundred years ago. The block itself is remarkable, but more wonderful still is the clear proof which its elaborate carvings give of Aztec civilization and enlightenment. This was their Calendar Stone on which a figure, carved in the centre, indicated the sun, while those which encircle it symbolized the months and days of the Aztec year, which was divided into eighteen months of twenty days each, with five complementary days added so as to make three hundred and sixty-five ; and once in fifty years they are said to have allowed for the loss of minutes in their reckoning.

Nevertheless, the Aztecs were a curious combination of intelligence and barbarism. Close beside this intricate sun calendar, for example, stands a hideous idol nine feet high. It is the image of their God of War, and was the principal object pointed out to Cortez by Montezuma when

THE AZTEC CALENDAR.

he revealed to him the Aztec temple. It was then covered with gold ornaments and jewels, and on the ground before it was a pan of incense containing several human hearts, since to this horrible deity thousands of lives were annually offered. The number of these victims seems incredible. It is supposed that the yearly sacrifices throughout the Aztec empire numbered no less than twenty thousand ; but reduce that estimate even one-half, and the result is appalling.

Remembering these facts, we shuddered as we looked upon the Sacrificial Stone which is, perhaps, the most horrible souvenir of priestly power and human cruelty that the world contains.   It once stood on the summit of the Aztec temple which was, as usual, in the form of a pyramid.   There, in the presence of the God of War, and altars never left without their sacred fire, rose this mysterious block of sacrifice.   It is a solid mass of polished porphyry, nine feet in diameter and three feet high, with top and sides profusely carved with likenesses of kings, and signs whose meaning is not clearly known; but one sad fact is plain enough.   In the centre of the block is a skull-shaped cavity, from which extends a channel to the outer edge.   Within that cavity the victim's head was placed as he lay outstretched upon the stone.   Five priests then held his head and limbs, while a sixth, arrayed in scarlet robes, cut open the victim's breast with a sharp, razor-like instrument, and drew forth the still warm and quivering heart.   This he at first held up in triumph, then laid it down before the statue of the god, while thousands in the square beneath bowed low in fear and adoration. Meantime, down the deep channel chiseled in the stone flowed a red stream of sacrificial blood, a terrible libation to the angry deity.   It is said that twelve thousand prisoners were sacrificed upon this block, at its dedication, in 1510.

AZTEC IDOL.

On leaving the Museum, we made our way to a charitable institution called the Hospital of Jesus, — a building founded by Cortez on the very spot where Montezuma for the first time grasped the Spaniard's hand, and bade him welcome to his capital.   It is worth remembering, in these days of will-breaking, that this old hospital is still maintained by the endowment bequeathed to it by the Conqueror, in spite of many attempts

THE SACRIFICIAL STONE AND IDOL.

by governments and private individuals to annul the legacy. Reflecting on the sad events which quickly followed the meeting here of Cortez and the Aztec king, we climbed a stairway to the second story of the building, and gazed upon the only authentic painting of Hernando Cortez which exists in Mexico It is not much to look at as a work of art, but it affords abundant food for thought, as one surveys those resolute features, in the very building founded by him centuries ago. With all

THE HOSPITAL OF JESUS.

his faults and cruelties, what energy and courage he possessed, what insight into human nature, and what a firm, indomitable will! The story of the Conquest reads like a romance. Though he had only a few hundred men, in two weeks after entering the Aztec capital Cortez had caused the sovereign, Montezuma, to be seized and held a prisoner, had captured the Aztec treasury, valued at six and a half million dollars, and had ordered many of Montezuma's ministers, who had counseled opposition

THE PAINTING OF CORTEZ.

to the invaders, to be burned to death. A few weeks later the broken-hearted Montezuma also died, despised by those who had formerly trembled at his glance.

We saw in the hospital the standard which the followers of Cortez bore through many desperate conflicts. Over what dreadful scenes of carnage has this banner floated! For the Aztec nation was not easily subdued. The armor of the Spaniards, and the sight for the first time of horses and cannon, took them by surprise; but when the invaders tried to burn their temples, and offered violence to their gods, the Aztec's national pride was touched beyond all power of control, and they arose *en masse* to rescue their country from invasion and their shrines from sacrilege. They were content to lose a thousand lives from their own ranks, if they could shed the blood of a single Spaniard. "The

THE SACRED BANNER.

only trouble is," they proudly said, "there are too few of you to glut the vengeance of our gods!"

A mile or two outside the city stands a venerable cedar, known by the name of La Noche Triste, or "The Mournful Night." It was under this tree, on the eventful evening when the Spaniards retreated from the city, that even the iron resolution of Cortez failed him, and he wept bitterly at the seemingly overwhelming ruin which had come upon him. For, execrated and pursued by an appailing multitude of Aztecs, the Spaniards had been

THE MOURNFUL NIGHT TREE.

THE PASEO.

STATUE OF GUATEMOZIN.

driven from the capital, fighting for life at every step, bleeding from countless wounds, and, apparently, destined to be massacred ere they could reach the coast. In view of the cruelty and bloodshed which they subsequently caused, it seems almost a pity that they did not all perish. Within a year, however, they had returned, and regained everything that had been lost.

Extending westward from the City of Mexico, is a magnificent avenue called the Paseo. This is a feature of their capital of which the Mexicans may justly feel proud, although they are indebted for it to the Emperor Maximilian. It is a noble boulevard, fully two hundred feet in breadth, and straight as an arrow for two miles. On either side are double rows of shade trees, beneath which stroll the multitudes who must content themselves with merely gazing at the brilliant spectacle of carriages and horses, as the fashionable world of Mexico sweeps by. At intervals, this driveway is embellished by six circular spaces intended for the statues of distinguished men. Some of these are already occupied; and that which most attracted me was the monument of Guatemozin, the nephew of Montezuma, and the last of the Aztec emperors. Few men have better merited a bronze memorial than this undaunted hero of a vanquished race. When he knew that his cause was absolutely hopeless, when Montezuma had expired, and the capital had become a vast charnel house, in which the invading Spaniards, sick at last of slaughter, could hardly take a step save on the body of an Indian, this Aztec king rejected every summons to surrender; and, finally, when taken prisoner on the last foot of soil which remained to him, he looked his conqueror, Cortez, proudly in the face and said: "I have done all I could to save my people, but have failed. Draw, then, that dagger from your belt and set me free!" Cortez, however, filled with admiration, did not strike the blow, although it would have been more merciful if he had done so then and there; for when the lust for gold had driven nobler feelings from the Conqueror's breast, he shamefully allowed the brave young Emperor to be tortured, in the vain attempt to force him to reveal the hiding-place of the Aztec treasures. Though his feet were soaked in oil, and he was suspended over a slow fire, no amount of suffering caused Guatemozin to betray his secret. The hidden treasure was never discovered, and though the deposed Emperor survived his torture, he was finally hanged by the command of Cortez.

CASTLE OF CHAPULTEPEC.

BIG TREES AT CHAPULTEPEC.

Reaching the limit of the avenue, we found ourselves before a rocky, isolated hill about two hundred feet in height. It was the world-renowned Chapultepec, — the favorite residence of Mexican rulers from Montezuma down to President Diaz. The present palace on its summit has no great antiquity, but the majestic cypresses around its base are many centuries old, and have cast their shadows impartially upon the Aztec and the Austrian, the conqueror and the conquered. In any portion of the world, apart from their historic associations, these trees would call forth admiration; for some of them are sixty feet in circumference, and Humboldt thought that one, at least, had an age of sixteen hundred years. It seems appropriate, therefore, that these monarchs of the past should wear, to-day, long pendent veils of soft gray moss, as if in mourning for the line of kings whose gardens once extended far beyond this hill. Per-

THE TREE OF MONTEZUMA

chance they also mourn their lost companions; for thousands
of the trees between Chapultepec and Mexico were cut down
by the Spaniards for material to rebuild the city which, in
their final desperate conflict with the Aztecs, they had
totally destroyed.

The finest of these arboreal giants is called the Tree of
Montezuma. I felt myself a pygmy as I stood beside it, not
merely in comparison with its gigantic form, but as I measured
my brief life with the long series of eventful centuries, of
whose slow march its gnarled and twisted limbs gave proof.
This cypress may have flourished here before a human voice
disturbed the silence of this grove, or a human foot was
pressed upon the soil of Mexico. At all events, there is no
doubt that it has sheltered Aztec princes glittering in bar-
baric splendor, and has looked down for centuries on Spanish
cavaliers, sandaled monks, and beautiful Castilian ladies rendered
still lovelier by their lace mantillas. American soldiers, too,
have marched   beneath its
sturdy   limbs,

MONUMENT TO MEXICAN CADETS.

A MEXICAN VALLEY VIEW.

to be succeeded in their turn by French Zouaves; while, mournfully conspicuous in the historic throng above which its gray moss has waved its welcome and farewell, appeared the Austrian sovereigns, Maximilian and Carlotta, — ill-fated victims of Napoleon's dream of empire in the Western hemisphere.

The view from the summit of Chapultepec is one of the most beautiful in the world. Stretching away from the base of the hill lies an almost circular valley, forty-five miles in length and thirty-five in breadth. It is as level as a tranquil sea, and is surrounded by a mountain wall, which Nature seems to have raised around it to protect her favorite. What wonder that this view has captivated every conqueror who has beheld it? For, in the centre of this lofty plain, and girdled by empurpled mountains, like a gem encircled by a ring of amethysts, glitters the City of the Montezumas, — Mexico.

Two of these mountains are the extinct volcanoes, Popocatepetl and Iztaccihuatl, whose summits reach a height of nearly eighteen thousand feet. It is not strange that the Aztecs regarded them with superstitious awe and reverence, especially, as in their day, and even at the period of the Conquest, the action of Popocatepetl was at times extremely violent. Indeed, the

MOUNT POPOCATEPETL.

name of Popocatepetl signifies "The Smoking Mountain," though, during the present century, the title has hardly been justified. Quite naturally, however, in the period of its activity the Aztecs deemed it the abode of tortured spirits, whose agonies within their fiery prison-house caused the terrific groaning of the mountain previous to an eruption, and, finally, the dreadful outburst of its flames and smoke. Until the coming of the Spaniards, no one had dared to ascend it; but the followers of Cortez, laughing to scorn the warnings of the Aztecs, made an attempt to climb it and succeeded. One of the party chosen by lot was lowered from the crater's edge four hundred feet into the horrible abyss, where he filled baskets with sulphur to be used in the manufacture of gunpowder. Strange, is it not? The violence of Popocatepetl ceased soon after the arrival of the Spaniards, but probably that deadly gift of sulphur proved far more fatal to the Aztecs than all the previous outbursts that had marked its history.

BURRO TRAIN.

Iztaccihuatl, or "The White Woman," derives its name from
the fact that its form resembles that of a dead woman robed in
white for burial. From some points of view the likeness is
startling. The head appears to fall back, as in death; and
from this lines of snow, like long disheveled silvery tresses,
stream in all directions. An Indian tradition says that these
volcanoes were once living beings, a giant and a giantess; but

IZTACCIHUATL.

that the Deity, angered by their haughty independence, trans-
formed them into mountains. The woman died at once and
lies outstretched forever in a winding sheet of snow. Her
lover, far less fortunate, is doomed to live in full view of her
lifeless body; and when his sorrow becomes uncontrollable, he
shakes the earth in his convulsive grief and pours forth tears of
fire.

Saying farewell one morning to the capital we started to
explore the temperate and tropic lands of Mexico, which lie

THE TRAIN FOR VERA CRUZ.

between the ocean and the table-land, bathed in perpetual sunshine, and rivaling in beauty and luxuriance the golden gardens of Hesperides. In a few hours we had reached the edge of the great Mexican plateau, and, with some trepidation, began the won-derful journey toward Vera Cruz. I rightly call it wonderful, for the railway by which it is accomplished is one of the most remarkable specimens of engineering skill and courage that the world can show. Most of the descent of eight thousand feet is made in about twenty miles. The steepness of the track can, therefore, be imagined. Railroad grades seldom exceed a fall of one foot in a hundred ; but here there is at times

DOUBLE-HEADED ENGINE.

an incline of four feet in a hundred. Standing on the rear platform, we experienced the sensation of *sliding* down the mountains, and it seemed wonderful that the heavy train did not rush downward to destruction. What kept it from so doing was a monstrous double engine, used, not only to pull its heavy burdens up the mountains, but also to restrain them in the descent. When necessity requires it, one-half of the engine works in a direction opposite to that in

A CURVING BRIDGE.

which the train is moving, in order to retard the almost overwhelming force of gravitation. It is a serious undertaking; for any undue impetus on the edge of these stupendous cliffs would mean swift death to every one on board. Few accidents, however, have occurred; no doubt because they are so constantly anticipated. It is where men are heedless from a sense of perfect safety that real danger lies; not in the iron bridge watched carefully from hour to hour, but in the little culvert or the loosened rail

I was astonished to perceive that though a brakeman stood on every car there were no air-brakes on our train. "We could not keep them," was the explanation. "As fast as we put them on, the natives, who are inveterate thieves, cut them off and carried them away. In fact, until we riveted the spikes that hold down the rails, they stole them also; and rubber pads

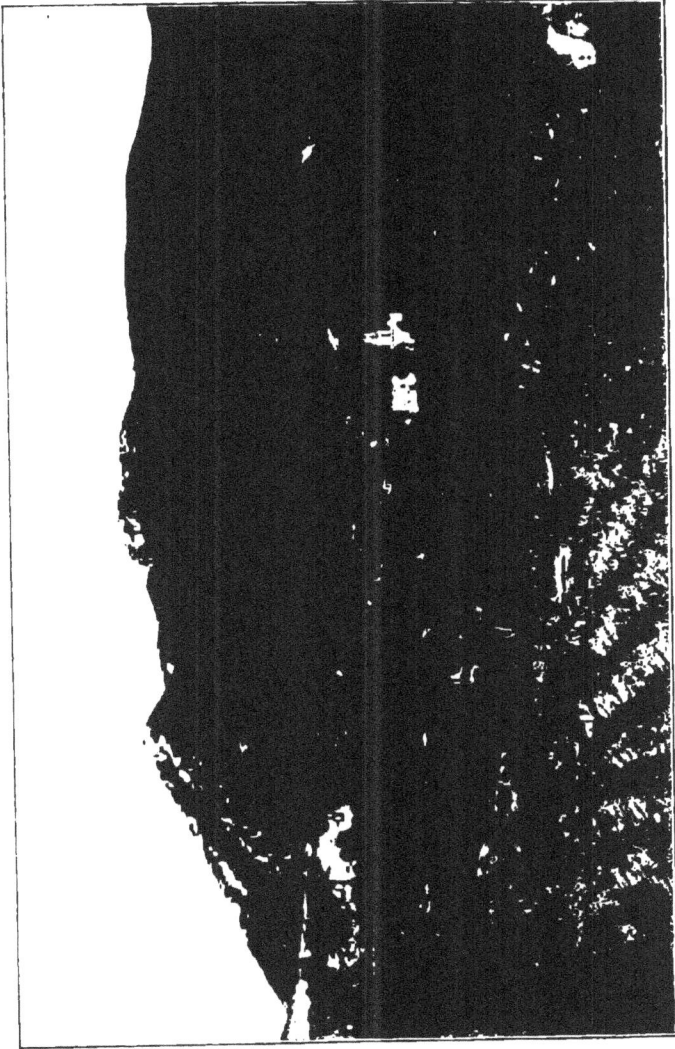

A MEXICAN VALLEY.

on the steps of Pullman cars invariably suffered the same fate."
I noticed that steel ties were used instead of wooden ones, and
that the sides of the cars were made
of corrugated
iron ; since it
is claimed that
wood will not
endure the sud-
den changes,
daily, from the

A MEXICAN OX-CART.

intense heat of the tropics to the cooler table-land.

The scenery on this route is magnificent. At times we saw
a broad expanse of cultivated fields three thousand feet below
us, the whitewashed buildings on their surface resembling
dice upon a checker-board. The trees looked so diminutive,
that they recalled the tiny playthings of our childhood called
"Swiss Villages." At one point, the descent was so precipitous, that the Indians, who had been selling fruit and flowers
at a station half up the mountain, ran down the rocks and
reached another halting-place before our train arrived, and were
ready to renew
their traffic. A
characteristic feat-
ure of this railway
journey was the
variety of life and
merchandise dis-
cernible at every
station. No sooner
would we halt than
scores of dark-
hued men and
women swarmed
about the cars,

SCENERY ON THE VERA CRUZ RAILWAY.

crying their wares in harsh, discordant tones which sounded
like a chorus of creaking signs on a windy night. The number
of these Indian traders, the miscellaneous objects which they
sold, and above all the amount of necessary bargaining, in
broken English and Spanish spoken on the installment plan,
were both novel and amusing. Every part of Mexico seems
to have a special article to tempt the tourist. In one place
oranges are sold, the next produces baskets of all shapes and
sizes; at Irapuato strawberries are offered every day, the whole
year round; another place is famous for its handsome canes;
another still, for opals or for onyx. Everywhere we heard
the cry of "Pulque! Pulque!" and had that nauseating mixture
offered us by hands that looked more uninviting than the drink
itself, — all mute, inglorious witnesses of the scarcity of soap.

At length we reached our destination for the night, the
little town of Orizaba. It was the edge of evening when we
strolled through its streets. The temperature was as high as
that of New York in July.   The air was heavy
with the odors of luxu-   riant vegeta-

FRUIT-SELLERS AT THE STATION.

THE ALAMEDA AT ORIZABA.

CORN-FIELD AND SLEEPING WATCHER.

tion. Occasionally a tufted palm outlined its graceful form against the sky; yet, even then, we were not really in the Hot Lands. Compared with Vera Cruz and its adjoining territory Orizaba is cold; and the inhabitants of the coast actually come to this elevation for relief from heat, and to escape yellow fever which is here unknown. Perpetual summer reigns along this Mexican terrace; not hot enough to make existence unendurable, yet with an air sufficiently relaxing to cause ambition to appear a farce, exertion an absurdity, and any special interest in life beyond a cup of coffee, the aroma of a fine cigar, the music of a mandolin, and

FARMER BOYS, ORIZABA.

the smile of a fair señora, not worth the trouble that it costs. Yes, if there be a district in the world especially adapted to a life of *dolce far niente*, it is the natural terrace on which lie the little towns of Cordova and Orizaba, filled with the fragrance of magnificently timbered forests, and situated equidistant from a plain of almost equatorial heat and the cool shadows of Chapultepec.

On the Vera Cruz railway we traveled no further toward the coast than Orizaba, because the health officials had informed us that if our car descended to the Hot Lands, we should be quarantined

THE HAND-CARS.

on our return. Moreover, although this route is best adapted for a view of Mexico's temperate zone, in order to really see the tropics, another grand descent is preferable, along the recently completed railroad down the mountains to Tampico. Accordingly, we made our way to a different point on the edge of the Mexican plateau, prepared this time to take a plunge into the real Tierras Calientes.

It was seven o'clock in the morning when we left our car, and, on the brink of the great table-land, seated ourselves on vehicles, which, though much larger than our ordinary hand-

TUNNEL ON THE ROUTE TO TAMPICO.

cars, nevertheless resembled them. Two benches crossed each, one in the front the other in the rear, and in the space between was a heavy brake, upon the strength of which the safety of our lives depended ; for we were now, by the force of gravity alone, to slide down from the temperate to the torrid zone, upon a curving track, in places steeper than the road to Vera Cruz. Of course, we might have taken a regular train upon this route, but from no ordinary conveyance could we have viewed and photographed the scenery to such advantage as from these open cars. The difference was as great as that between riding in a covered barouche and in

RAILROAD TO TAMPICO.

an open wagon. There was no danger of a collision, for we had seen the telegraphic order sent to hold the up-train at the base of the mountain till we should arrive. " Had the instructions been received and understood ? " " Click, click, click," came the reassuring answer. It was all right ; the track was clear, and it belonged to us. *Vamanos !* The ride that followed was incomparably the most exciting of my life. Now we went dashing through a tunnel which had a temperature as cooling as a shower-bath, or whirling round a precipice upon a shelf of rock, beneath which was a gorge two thousand feet in depth; a moment later, we would slide in a straight line along the glittering grooves with a momentum that would have been frightful, but for the steady hand maintained upon the brake. Even when thus controlled, it seemed at times as if the car were actually alive and leaping forward on the rails like a thoroughbred on the race-track; for we were making a descent of seven thousand feet in fifteen miles, including the windings of the track. I must confess that there

DOWN THE TRACK.

were moments when I felt a little nervous, and once, when we had attained a speed that made a gentleman from Chicago turn pale and raise his eyes toward heaven, as if considering what his chances were of going there, I called a halt and took some photographs. The railroad winds about the mountains in tremendous loops, like a gigantic serpent. Compared with many feats of engineering here, the famous Pennsylvania Horseshoe Bend sinks into insignificance. The scenery was glorious. The mountains, glistening to their summits with luxuriant vegetation, appeared to be covered with soft, velvet mantles. At times we heard that rare and most delightful sound in Mexico, — the music of a waterfall.

"What is that?" I presently inquired, turning my field-

SCENERY ON THE TAMPICO ROUTE

glass toward a mountain summit far above us, "can a farm
be located at such a height?"

"Yes," said our guide, "it is a corn plantation, and a
good one too."

"But how can
it be cultivated?"

"Well," said
the man, with a
twinkle in his
eye, "no one can
really climb there
to work it; but
the owner
plants

SCENERY NEAR TAMPICO.

POOL AND FOUNTAIN, NEAR LAS PALMAS.

it from a distance
by firing the seed
from a shotgun;
and, when the corn
ripens in the fall, he
harvests the crop with
a rifle. You see the bul-
lets cut the stalks, and,
naturally, the ears of corn
at once fall down the perpendicular cliffs!"

Around and below us, as far as the eye could reach, lay
a vast ocean of intensely colored foliage. Sometimes a powerful field-glass separated this into plantations of bananas, coffee, sugar-cane, and cotton; in other places, Nature reigned

supreme in jungles tenanted by Mexican tigers, lions, monkeys, and hyenas. At length our track grew level. This fact alone would have assured us we had reached the Hot Lands, even if the oppressive

NEAR LAS PALMAS.

heat and tropical vegetation had left any room to doubt it. Here, birds of brilliant plumage frequently darted back and forth above our heads in startling numbers and astonishing variety. It is a region marvelously endowed by Nature. Its

forests hold choice cabinet woods, in such profusion that mahogany ties are frequently used upon the railroad. The mountains, also, yield a vast amount of onyx, agate, and black marble. The American owner of an onyx mine in the vicinity assured me that although he had employed only fifteen men five years before, he then had a pay-roll of five hundred, and was sending onyx, not only to the City of Mexico, but to New York, Paris, Berlin, and St. Petersburg. Tobacco, too, is indigenous to this country, and was used in the halls of Montezuma long before the time of Cortez. In fact, as is well known, the tobacco plant derives its name from Tabaco, a place in Yucatan.

I doubt if there is anything more primitive and unconventional among the Hottentots than the homes and costumes of the Indians of the Mexican Hot Lands. Their wretched dwellings are not as

"INNOCENT OF DRESS."

substantial as the adobe huts of the plateau, but are composed of barrel staves, old railroad ties, sugar-cane stalks, pieces of matting, or even palm leaves. The bare ground usually serves the inmates for a bed, and the amount of clothing visible on the men and women is astonishingly scanty. The children walk about as innocent of dress as Raphael's cherubs. We occasionally saw articles of attire hung upon a line, but they belonged to the "section men" (usually Americans) employed along the railroad; for taking in washing is one way in which these Indians earn a liveli-

hood.   Another is the transportation of great burdens on their
backs, and what they can accomplish in the way of burden-
bearing is almost incredible.   Many of them will carry heavy
loads forty-five miles in a single day, and as a rule will surpass
a horse in endurance.   Their hair is usually left thick above
their eyes, to serve as a matting for the strap which holds the
load, and thus, with bowed heads, they will go as fast as a horse
can walk.   This is not a new characteristic of the Mexican

HEAVILY LOADED.

Indians.
Before the Conquest let-
ters were carried through
the Aztec empire by swift-footed cou-
riers, the distance between Vera Cruz
and Mexico (about two hundred miles), being traversed
in twenty-four hours.   Such messages were, generally, trans-
mitted in picture writings traced on cloth made from the
Maguey plant; and in this manner Montezuma was informed
of the landing of Cortez and his warriors on the coast.

One of the most enjoyable excursions that I made in Mexico
was to the ancient Pyramid of Cholula.   It does not look

pyramidal at present, but appears to be merely a natural hill two hundred feet in height. Yet, though to-day irregular in shape and covered with vegetation, it was originally the work of man, and formed a mighty pyramid, upon the top of which stood an imposing temple. Un-

PYRAMID OF CHOLULA.

der the hollow covering of earth that has collected upon its surface, it is composed of layers of clay and sun-dried bricks, which formed a solid mass, the base of which occupied no less than forty-five acres, while the summit reached a height of two

INTERIOR OF CHURCH, CHOLULA.

hundred feet. The amount of labor here involved is almost inconceivable. "Did it, then, rank with the great Pyramids of Egypt?" one naturally inquires. In one sense, yes; for

the enormous area of its base was larger; but, on the other
hand, its height was not one-half as great as that of Cheops,
or of Cephren, nor can its layers of bricks (though numbered
here by millions) produce at all the same impression as do
the mighty monoliths that make up the Egyptian pyramids,
reared by an almost superhuman power beside the Nile.

GIVING TO TWO AT ONCE.

Reaching the summit of Cholula's ancient mound, we stood
before the pretty church erected there. "The King is dead,
long live the King!" One deity has been dethroned, another
reigns here in his place. A Christian shrine now stands upon
the Aztec pyramid, much as in Rome the statue of St. Peter
surmounts the column of Trajan. Yet it would seem as if the
deities thus expelled had left their curse upon the place, for
only crumbling shrines and wretched hovels remain in the poor
village of Cholula which, nevertheless, in the time of Cortez was
the most sacred of all Indian towns, — the Mecca of the Aztecs.

Looking southward, a wonderful feature of the valley met our gaze in the silvery dome of Popocatepetl — a pyramid of God, beside which all the works of man dwindle to insignificance. One never tires of this majestic peak. For ages it has made the

A PUBLIC PATH.

landscape glorious, whether glowing with volcanic fires, or standing in god-like dignity, wrapped in its mantle of eternal snow; and while empires, dynasties, and races have lived their little lives, like insects, at its base, it has remained, in Nature's realm, the real, incomparable, God-appointed sovereign of Mexico.

VIEW FROM CHOLULA.

Whatever else of Mexico may be forgotten, I shall remember to my latest breath that wonderfully impressive vision from Cholula. Before me rose, against the darkening sky, a mighty cross, the sculptured proof that here Christianity had proved victorious; and as I lingered, my feet upon the Aztec pyramid, my hand upon the symbol of the conquerors' faith, my eyes turned toward that everlasting pinnacle of snow, I thought the lesson of Cholula to be this: that higher, grander, and far more enduring than all the different religions of humanity is the Eternal Power they imperfectly reveal; and that above the temples, pyramids, and crosses, which mark the blood-stained pathway of our race, rises a lofty mountain peak, whose glory falls alike upon the Aztec and the Spaniard, and in whose heaven-born radiance all races and all centuries may find their inspiration and their hope.

www.ingramcontent.com/pod-product-compliance
Lightning Source LLC
Chambersburg PA
CBHW021121270326
41929CB00009B/985